NO GRAVE
FOR
GRACE

A MEMOIR OF MYSTERY, MISSION,
AND MIRACLES

BY JUNIOR OBRAND

ISBN: 979-8-9932036-9-0 (Paperback)

Cover design by 846 Publishing
Cover photo by Driftwood Media

First Edition

Dedication

This book is for those who believed in me before I had any reason to believe in myself. To my parents, Esther Jacotin and my late father, Accevil Obrand, everything I've become started with you. I don't know how you managed to give so much with so little, but somehow, you did. Growing up in Pianotte, I could never have imagined the life I have now. I often describe my life as a statistical abnormality. In addition to God's grace, your quiet sacrifices made it possible. Dad, I carry you with me every day.

To the teachers who showed up at just the right time, Renald Duverslin, thank you for teaching me how to read. That simple gift opened up the world. Michel Jean Obner, you were the first to introduce me to English, and you did it with such patience and care.

Mike Mahowald, what you gave me wasn't just an education. Your decision to sponsor my schooling gave me a real shot. That kind of generosity echoes through generations, and I'll never forget it.

To my siblings, the Obrand crew. All ten of us faced tough times and got through them together. You taught me what it means to be strong, not in a loud way, but in the way that counts: getting back up, staying close, and holding each other up. I love you all more than I know how to say.

And to Paula, the love of my life, and our two children, Esther and Wesley, your presence was the final piece of the puzzle that gave my life its full meaning.

If you were to look up the word *'grave'* in a dictionary, you would probably encounter a definition resembling this:

Grave: noun (grāv): a place of burial for a dead body, typically a hole dug in the ground and marked by a stone or monument.

But for those of us who've seen life emerge from low places, we might define it differently:

The soil where silence waits. A resting place, not for endings, but for beginnings still hidden. What seems forgotten is only preparing to rise. Some things need the dark before they reach the light.

If you were to look up the word *'grace'* in a dictionary, you would probably encounter a definition resembling this:

Grace: noun (grās): unmerited divine assistance given to humans for their regeneration or sanctification.

But for those of us fortunate enough to live under the power of grace, we might define it differently:

Heaven's eraser, smoothing the rough drafts of your soul, even when your story is well-worn. It's that divine, ethereal space you live in, where you're blessed not because you're worthy, but because you're loved.

Pronunciation Guide

- **Gris-Gris:** Gree-Gree

- **Pianotte:** PEA-ya-note

- **Accevil:** AXE-say-ville

- **Sisal:** SEA-saul

- **Asèn:** AH-Saine

- **Regine**: Ray-JEAN

- **Cité Soleil:** See-TAY Soh-LEY

- **Aristide:** AR-reese-steed

- **Carrefour**: Car-FOOR

- **La Plaine:** Lah-Plehn

Praise for *No Grave for Grace*

"Junior Obrand is an inspiration. World-impacting adventures like his don't happen by chance. His story is shaped by his great faith and resilience, and by the faith and resilience of those who joined him on the journey. Just as Junior's life impacts everyone around him, his story will inspire you to write your own with` purpose and meaning."

—**J.J. Slag**, CEO of Feed My Starving Children

"It is a pleasure to commend the life and outreach of Junior Obrand. As one of the leaders of Feed My Starving Children, he has played a role in feeding millions of children around the world. He has served with a heart full of humility and a passion for giving children and their families a brighter future. His story, *No Grave for Grace*, is both compelling and remarkable."

—**Hal Donaldson**, President and Founder of Convoy of Hope; Author of *Your Next 24 Hours, Disruptive Compassion* & many more.

"Wow! I am utterly captivated by *No Grave for Grace*. This powerful, gritty narrative takes us through unimaginable escapes from poverty, death, and danger, shining a light on Junior's awe-inspiring, overcoming faith. His journey from hunger and peril to feeding the hungry worldwide is a miracle. These stories are so gripping and miraculous I'd doubt them without knowing Junior personally. It reads like a divinely scripted movie, with God as director, author, and stunt coordinator! It's a heartening reminder that what seems like an ending is often a hidden beginning—read this and let it lift your own story to new heights."

—**Ryan Skoog,** Best-selling Author, *Lead with Prayer* and Co-Founder/President VENTURE.ORG

"I have known Junior and his family for more than fifteen years. As a son of Gris-Gris, he embodies what it means to give back to his roots and his community. His journey from a young boy growing up in Haiti to traveling the world, holding hands with those in need, is a powerful testament to redemption and hope. In his memoir, *No Grave for Grace*, I know you'll find a chapter, a page, or a paragraph that resonates deeply. There is no doubt his story will inspire many more *'Juniors.'* You will quickly realize that this is not just Junior's story. It is a story that retraces the footsteps of hope and resilience. Happy reading!"

—**Father Fayant Cazeau,** Lead Pastor of Saint Rose of Lima, Gris-Gris, Haiti

"I had the privilege of meeting Junior Obrand two decades ago in the picturesque village of Gris-Gris, Haiti, where the beauty of the landscape blends seamlessly with the complexity of its history and culture. Through Junior's story, you'll discover how faith and hope can guide us through life's toughest challenges. *No Grave for Grace* unfolds like a puzzle, rich in narrative, layered with meaning, and ultimately inspiring. This book is a powerful reminder that every obstacle is an opportunity for growth. A must-read for anyone seeking inspiration and encouragement on their own life journey."

—**Ricardo Balmir,** Fellow Lead Haitian Professional Interpreter, longtime friend and colleague of the author

"Junior is the real deal: authentic, empathetic, kind, and gracious. He is a man who knows the grace of God, combining it with a grit forged through tough experiences and a gentleness born of a life spent serving others. We've worked, traveled, and broken bread together, and I've had the privilege of hearing his stories firsthand. Told with passion, conviction, and vulnerability, *No Grave for Grace* is truly life changing. I believe his story will impact your life as it has mine. That's why I'm so grateful Junior has taken the time to write this book and bless us all in doing so."

—**Isak Pretorius,** Group CEO of ForAfrika and Chief Evangelism Officer at Jesus Alive Gospel Outreach

"As a dear friend, I want to congratulate Junior on completing his memoir. After reading it, I realized this book is a powerful example of how God's grace moves in our lives. Page after page, you will see that even in the hardest moments, grace remains the one gift we can always depend on from above. When I finished *No Grave for Grace*, I came away with a deeper sense of life, grace, and mercy. You are in for a true gift! Enjoy it."

—**Moises Sifren,** President of Maranatha Mission, Dominican Republic

"Junior Obrand's *No Grave for Grace* is a moving testament to the strength of the human spirit and the guiding hand of grace. From the hills of Haiti to his role as a global advocate, Junior's journey shines with perseverance, humor, and faith. His story is both personal and universal, reminding us that even in hardship, grace can open paths we never imagined. I urge you to step into the pages ahead with open hearts and curious minds. This memoir is more than a life story; it is an invitation to reflect, to hope, and to embrace the light within our own journeys."

—**Etzer Emile,** MBA, Economist; Author, and President of Fondation Avenir, Port-au-Prince, Haiti

"Junior's story is not a Haitian story. It is not an American story. It is a human story of resilience. Like Joseph in the Bible, God used every challenge of childhood and every career fork in the road to turn whatever the devil meant for evil into something good, for the saving of many lives (Genesis 50:20)"

—**Edward Gary Brown,** Vice President of World Vision USA; Author of *From the Forbidden Fruit to the Final Feast*

"I have worked with Junior for over a decade. His faith, love of family, and dedication to feeding God's children will stir your heart and inspire you to take action. *No Grave for Grace* will lift and strengthen your spirit. Junior's story is one of resilience and the power of one person with an eternal perspective. *No Grave for Grace* will challenge you, humble you, and make you laugh. It will fill you with a resolve to do something greater for the least among us."

—**Mark Crea,** Former CEO of Feed My Starving Children.

"*No Grave for Grace* is a stirring journey of resilience, where hardship becomes the soil from which wisdom, joy, and hope take root. Junior's story and storytelling shine with courage, adventure, and the truth that—even in our darkest moments—light can break through. This memoir will inspire anyone who seeks to find meaning along life's unpredictable road, and it reminds us that with faith and grace, no obstacle or failure need ever be final."

—**Stefan Radelich,** CEO of LeSEA Global Feed
The Hungry

TABLE OF CONTENTS

Preface

The idea of writing this book had lingered in the back of my mind for nearly a decade. I'd always believed that a story left untold is like a gift left unwrapped, its potential never fully realized.

The decision to finally put words on paper came in the late spring of 2023. It was a beautiful day in May when several of my colleagues and I gathered in a conference room in Eagan, Minnesota, for a regularly scheduled meeting. Being a Christian organization, it was customary to begin each meeting with a devotion. But that morning's devotion posed a question I had never heard in that setting before: *"What would you do if you knew you could not fail?"*

We were each given three to five minutes to reflect and formulate our responses. My answer came to me before I could even grab a pen, fast and clear. When it was my turn to share, my five-word response was simple yet deeply genuine: "I would write a book."

Several of my colleagues replied with an even shorter question: "Why not?"

That afternoon, I decided to begin.

I grew up in a small village called Gris-Gris, nestled in the hills of Haiti, about 105 miles from Port-au-Prince. To my siblings and me (there were ten of us), it wasn't just a village. It was all we knew. It was our entire world.

Gris-Gris was so remote that stories from the city, especially from Port-au-Prince, the capital, felt like tales from another planet. Visitors returning from the city would captivate us with descriptions of streetlights, "lights on trees," they called them, and modern luxuries like electricity, televisions, and refrigerators, which we generically referred to as *Frigidaire*. Living in or even visiting Port-au-Prince was a status symbol, a dream for many in our village.

The journey to Gris-Gris was as rugged as the lives we lived there. The road was bumpy, strewn with rocks, and difficult to navigate. It was an adventure in itself. It wound around the village like a chaotic, hand-drawn sketch, carved by generations of footsteps and wear. After a rainstorm, it transformed into a muddy obstacle course, daring anyone brave enough to traverse it.

In the early to mid-1990s, traveling from Gris-Gris to Port-au-Prince took anywhere from eighteen to twenty-four hours. The first twenty-five miles had to be covered on foot, just to reach the official tap-tap station. Tap-taps are Haiti's most popular way to get around. Pickup trucks and small buses are refitted with benches, painted in bold colors, and often play loud Haitian music. The name comes from the custom of passengers tapping the side or back of the vehicle to signal when they want to get off.

Cars rarely came through Gris-Gris. When they did, they moved cautiously, dodging rocks, livestock, wandering children, and the occasional defiant chicken. Walking wasn't much easier; every step felt like an obstacle course. But for us, it was simply life. We knew those roads like we knew our own names.

Despite the hardships, Gris-Gris was stunningly beautiful. The winding gravel roads revealed green hills dotted with tiny, colorful houses clinging to the mountainsides. Palm trees swayed gently in the breeze, and the air was often filled with the tangy scent of sour oranges and limes. It was as if the land itself whispered a quiet reminder: "Yes, life is tough, but there's still beauty here."

For a village of 16,000 people, we had almost nothing—no running water, no electricity, no modern conveniences. There was no police station, no fire department. Only two people in the entire village owned cars: the Catholic priest and the village carpenter.

I'll never forget the first time I got to ride in a car. It was late afternoon when a red two-door Toyota got stuck in the mud. The driver went around asking for help to push it free. Some of my siblings and I eagerly jumped in to assist. It was the first car we'd ever touched up close, and I secretly wished it would stay stuck just a little longer so I could linger near it.

In less than 15 minutes, we had the car freed. The driver then invited us to hop in for a ride. For a barefoot kid who had only ever walked everywhere, the sound of the engine and the wind on my face felt like pure magic.

Sometimes, I marvel at how a kid from Gris-Gris, a place where opportunities were as rare as the money needed to chase them, has managed to find his way in a world so vastly different. Was I special? Did I have something others didn't? The answer is always the same: no. I owe my journey to two things: God's hand of grace and the tenacious love of my parents.

We weren't wealthy; far from it. But my parents gave us something far more valuable: love, faith, and hope. My mother always said, "The waves may be high, but our boat is secure." She taught us to face life's storms with courage. My father, with his quiet strength, showed us the value of perseverance. And my siblings? We laughed, dreamed, and leaned on each other, even when there wasn't enough food to fill our bellies.

I wasn't extraordinary. I was simply blessed with a family that taught me your starting point doesn't determine your destination. Gris-Gris didn't give me material wealth, but it gave me lessons, love, and memories that shaped the person I am today.

This book is a tribute to my parents. My father was our rock. My mother was, and still is, our heart and soul. We used to joke that she was "more Catholic than the Pope," and her faith ran deeper than anyone I've ever known.

Though she never attended school, my mother taught herself to read at age 50 so she could study the Bible on her own. She made sure we held education and faith in equal regard. I was her go-to Bible reader for the daily six a.m. prayer gatherings she hosted in our yard.

Life in Gris-Gris wasn't easy. Poverty was the norm, and many nights we went to bed hungry. Growing up, the idea of having three full meals in a single day felt extraordinary, not just for us Obrand kids, but for most families in town. It happened so rarely that we came up with our own word for it: a "touchdown."

The term had nothing to do with American football. In fact, I didn't know the first thing about football back then. Still, the word seemed to fit. On those rare days when there was breakfast, lunch, and dinner, someone would inevitably smile and say, "Looks like we got a touchdown today." And it always felt like a small victory.

I can't say for sure where the term originated, but it caught on. For years, my friends and I used it without thinking, a quiet way of acknowledging those rare moments when the table felt full, and so did we.

Money wasn't easy to come by, and there were no formal jobs where you could earn it either. Even a twenty-cent exam fee for school felt like an insurmountable challenge. Yet my mother always found ways to give. She'd set aside a bowl of food for a passerby, and on days when we had enough, she'd send a portion to Saint Jude's House, known as the Poor House in our village. Her faith in God and humanity remained unshaken, even when we questioned it.

There were times we asked her directly, "if God loves all His children, then why do some have food, clothes, and toys, while people like us have none?" She'd smile gently and reply, "the waves may be high, but our boat is secure."

This book is filled with stories of struggle and miracles, of a life shaped by God, by loving parents, and by events that defy logic. Some stories you'll read may challenge your thinking and trigger that familiar two-word response: no way. But I promise you, they're all true.

As you read the pages ahead, I invite you to pause and ask yourself: *What would you do if you knew you couldn't fail?* If the answer comes quickly, then your next question should be: Why not?

This book wasn't written with profit in mind. I wrote about my life story to reach you, to sit beside you, wherever you are, and offer a piece of my story that would make no sense except for God's grace. I'm not sharing it as a roadmap, but as a mirror. Along the way, you may find moments that inspire you, others that unsettle you, and maybe a few that echo something you've lived through yourself.

Like the roads in and around Gris-Gris, my journey hasn't followed a straight path. It's been more like a winding road at dusk, full of sharp turns I didn't see coming, detours that left me disoriented, and near-collisions I walked away from only by God's grace. There's no other explanation I can offer for some of the things I've made it through.

This isn't just my story. It's a reminder, especially if the waters in your life feel rough right now, that with the right foundation beneath you, you can endure the storm. I come from a place where resilience isn't a choice; it's stitched into our spirits. Haitians are experts at finding sunlight, even when the sky offers nothing but gray.

As you turn the pages ahead, I invite you in, not as a distant reader, but as a fellow sojourner. I hope that somewhere between the lines, something stirs in you. That you pause, even for a brief moment, and reflect on what we're really doing here during this short layover on Earth, on our way to eternity.

PART ONE

CHAPTER 1
Naming Rights

In the Caribbean Sea, when a hurricane is born, it's given a name. It's measured, tracked, and charted by those who study weather patterns for a living. But in rural Haitian villages like mine, where children grow up in the shadows of poverty, names come differently. And so do the storms that shape them.

In Haiti, names carry weight. They tell stories, mark history, hold the spirit of a place, or reflect the measure of a boy who will grow to be a man. When people ask where I'm from, I usually say "Haiti." But there's more to that answer. The truth is, I'm from a small town called Gris-Gris, a name most outsiders, even within Haiti, wouldn't recognize.

Gris-Gris isn't the kind of place you can just look up online. Put it in a GPS and you'll either get nothing or end up somewhere in France with a name that only sounds close. It's the kind of place you have to feel your way into. No street signs, no billboards announcing its name. Inside the so-called "town" of Gris-Gris were smaller pockets of life, neighborhoods within neighborhoods, and each had its own heartbeat.

My family came from one of those places, a little corner called Pianotte. It wasn't the kind of place people came looking for opportunity; it was the kind of place where you fought to create your own. For clarity and ease of reading, the names Pianotte and Gris-Gris will be used interchangeably throughout this book.

Pianotte didn't have a zip code. Our house wasn't tied to any street name. If you were trying to find the Obrand family residence, you had to rely on certain unconventional landmarks. Look for the big mahogany tree near the roadside, where a mother set up her cooking pot and a wooden table to sell marinade, crispy fried dough seasoned with chicken bouillon and onions.

On days when the pot stayed cold and no smoke curled from under the coconut tree-covered canopy, that same mother sold moonshine as clear as potable water. And if you happened to be looking for our house on a Sunday, you couldn't miss it. Right next to the mahogany tree sat a cockfighting ring, where the Sunday afternoon noise echoed through the neighborhood like a car with no muffler.

Our house had two numbers: 47 and 28, but the city didn't assign them. My older brother Joel assigned those numbers himself with a black, permanent Sharpie, and they weren't for mail delivery. They were for the lottery. In our town, if someone dreamed of our house, those numbers told them what to bet in the lottery. We had a system. It wasn't written down, and it wasn't taught in school. If you wanted to understand it, you had to ask one of us. It was family knowledge, passed down like a recipe.

My father, Accevil, had three daughters from his first marriage before he met my mother, Esther. Together, they had seven more children. If my father's name sounds unfamiliar, that's because it is. In all my years, I've never met another Accevil. The name itself was rare, just like the man who carried it.

He was a farmer by trade. He never had a formal education, as far as I know he never even set foot in a school, but that never defined his intelligence or work ethic. In his world, waking up after sunrise was an insult to the land. He used to say, "Never let the sun rise before you." And he meant it. For him, seeing sunshine as you opened your eyes was synonymous with laziness.

To this day, his voice still lingers in my head. Without fail, my eyes usually pop open at five a.m. It's as if my body is hardwired to this lesson. I don't fight it. Waking early is just another part of the inheritance he passed down, one that has

3

served me well. Before my father met my mother, he was married to Jeanitte (a name as unique as his own). Together, they had three daughters: Yole, Gougou, and Marie.

I should mention that in Haiti, nicknames are a rite of passage. No one calls you by your legal name unless you're in trouble. Yole's real name was Yolande, Marie was Huguette, and Gougou was Goureille. But if you didn't know that, you'd never guess.

Some nicknames in Haiti are logical, connected in some way to a person's given name. Others? They seem to come out of thin air, bestowed by an older relative or a neighbor who decided to call you something different one day, and that was that. It stuck, and it became the name you were called forever.

Growing up in Pianotte, names came in two flavors: the mysterious ones that seemed to carry secret messages only their name givers understood, and the wildly creative ones that left you wondering what inspired them. In third grade, for example, I had a classmate named *Dieukifel*, which literally translates as "It was God who did it." I thought that was one way to give credit where credit's due. Names like *Nawel*, meaning "we will see," and *Dieusibon*, meaning "God is so good," floated around too, each one carrying a little piece of hope, mystery, or wonder.

I didn't hear the full story about my name until I was a teenager. That was common in Pianotte. Like most kids, I had two names: the one everyone in and around the village called me, and the one printed on my birth certificate. Naming a child was the easy part. Getting that child registered in the eyes of the government, though, was like playing Bingo and crossing your fingers hoping for B5.

No one ever told me why, but in Pianotte my nickname was Asèn. Everyone used it, from parents to siblings, cousins, and neighbors. But in public, like the classroom, Asèn got folded up and tucked away while I stepped into my legal name. I sometimes think nicknames were a kind of quiet strategy. In Haiti, where registering a child always felt like an endless maze, a nickname was a simple gift that asked for nothing. You didn't need to complete any forms or purchase stamps, just a word and suddenly it was yours.

Let me share about the registration process of a child once they were born. Instead of a hospital recording the birth immediately, a government representative, known as a public notary, would make his way through the villages. He arrived as an official figure, trotting in on horseback, visiting each town on a set schedule. He reached our village once a month, always on a Wednesday.

He documented new births, writing down names, spelling them however he saw fit, and ensuring each child officially existed in the eyes of the government. It wasn't just first names he took liberties with; last names, too, were reshaped at his discretion. Sometimes they were stretched, sometimes trimmed, always with a purpose known only to him. The way he spelled them felt less like a mistake and more like a quiet assertion. As if names weren't fixed but living, flexible parts of a story he was still writing. Regardless of the spelling decided by the public notary, parents understood that names weren't just labels. They were stories, traditions, and, in some cases, hopes.

When my parents finally settled on my name, they waited for a Wednesday. They knew the notary would be in town, so they told him they wanted to call me Junior, simple and clear. But the notary had other plans. He took the name and gave it his own twist, as if he couldn't resist putting a personal stamp on it.

What ended up on the birth certificate was a version of "Junior" that made no logical sense. Letters were shuffled, a flourish added here and there. My parents never questioned it. My legal name, the one printed on my birth certificate, turned out to be so rare that I've never met another Jignore.

I didn't think much of it until I was a teenager, when classmates would ask, "How come it's spelled like that?" I figured it was the notary's executive decision. That was just the way things worked. So many people couldn't read, and there was no correcting his choices. In many towns across Haiti, that practice continues, where the spelling of a child's name often depends on the notary's mood that day.

Misspelling my first name never really bothered me. After all, Jignore is such a unique name, and it carries a story with it. What caught me off guard, though, was just how far the notary expanded his discretion. In my family, even our last name wasn't safe from confusion. Out of the ten of us, some birth certificates have Obrand, others Obran, and a few Aubrand or Aubran. We all share the same parents, the same roots, but on paper, you wouldn't always know it.

At first, it felt like an odd quirk, something we could laugh about at family gatherings. But over time, those little differences became bigger problems. There were moments, standing in government offices, trying to gather paperwork, when clerks would look at us like we were strangers to each other.

In Haiti, where getting any official document is already hard enough, mismatched last names can feel like a locked door. We've had to explain ourselves again and again, proving that yes, we're siblings, and yes, we belong to the same family. The names on our birth certificates don't always say so, but we know who we are. Still, the system doesn't always see it that way.

Naming traditions often followed religious customs. Since Haiti is predominantly Catholic, many children were named according to the Saint's feast day on which they were born. A baby born near March 19th might be named Joseph, in honor of St. Joseph's feast day. One born in late January might be named Paul, after the feast of St. Paul. In many cases, parents didn't choose their children's names at all, the calendar did.

But religion wasn't the only influence; soccer played a massive role, too. Even though my village had no electricity, no TV, and no access to live games, we still knew what was happening in the world of soccer, perhaps our favorite sport. News about soccer often came to us through people visiting from Port-au-Prince. By the time it reached our village, the rest of the world had already moved on, but to us, it still mattered. Every goal, every match meant a lot. The lag in news didn't weaken our love for the game. If anything, it made it feel more exciting, more alive, as if we were waiting for a secret that even people like us would come to know. Haitians are deeply passionate about the game. And despite never seeing the greats play, we grew up hearing about the legendary Brazilian and Argentinian players. Names like Romario, Diego (after Diego Maradona), Roberto, and Carlos became so popular that entire generations of Haitian boys were named after South American soccer stars.

Recounting the story of how my name was stamped on paper and recognized by the government is not a criticism against my parents. They were the textbook definition of hardworking people. My father rose with the sun and worked until it sank again, often with nothing more than a sip of water and a glass of moonshine to keep him going against the brutal Caribbean sun. When evening came and most men would rest, he would often go to the field behind our house, laboring until it was too dark to see his own hands.

For my father, life was about survival. He wasn't a man who dealt in luxury or even stability. He dealt in sisal. If you've never heard of sisal, you're not alone. It's a fibrous plant, sharp-edged and green like a massive aloe vera. But instead of healing burns, its value lay beneath the surface. When soaked in water for weeks, the tough outer skin would peel away to reveal strong, white fibers that could be woven into ropes, bags, twine, and other essentials.

In Pianotte, water wasn't just scarce, it was sacred. We treated it with reverence, almost like gold. Every drop mattered. There was no luxury of soaking the sisal to soften it. That meant we had to find another way, a method that didn't rely on what we didn't have. And so, like most things in that place, necessity shaped invention.

Our tools were humble but clever. One was a flat slab of wood, smoothed from years of use, which we called the banko. The other was the rap, a short, rounded wooden piece, easy to hold in the hand, with a strip of metal fixed to the bottom, sharpened just enough to grip and strip the tough fibers.

There was something rhythmic about the work: pressing the sisal against the banko, dragging the blade down in steady strokes. The sound it made still lives somewhere in the back of my mind.

It wasn't the kind of work that drew admiration. It was slow and repetitive, and the dry fibers could bite into your fingers after a while. But there was also something quiet and grounding in it. We weren't just peeling sisal; we were making do, bending hardship into a routine.

Sisal wasn't just a job. It was the job for us. At ten years old, I was handed the two main tools I'd need to start working in the sisal business. These were the tools that would help me scratch out a living and cover basic expenses, like school fees or buying a pen.

Scratching sisal wasn't just hard work; it also stole my sleep. You had to start early because once the sun came up, the heat made the work unbearable. If you tried scratching the green part of the sisal when it was too hot, you'd end up with a terrible itch and a skin rash. So by two a.m., we'd be up, scratching away, stopping only when the sun began to rise. Some of my siblings and I even used the stars as our clock, figuring it was time to get to work when they shone brightest in the sky.

We used to joke that working with sisal felt like a job where you had to dress for an important business meeting, pants and long sleeves, not to impress anyone, but to keep from getting scratched up by the plants. My father often reminded us that *travay se libète*, work is freedom.

Haiti and Mexico were the world's main producers of sisal, and my father saw an opportunity in it.

He wasn't just a farmer; he was a businessman, or at least as much of one as a man with no formal education and little to no capital could be in a place like Pianotte. Sisal offered a source of income, meager as it was. My father would buy sisal from farmers, resell it, and make a small profit by measuring the fibers by weight. Every kilo was worth five gourdes back then, about twenty cents.

A person could spend two weeks working endlessly, peeling sisal, and still end up with barely two dollars in his pocket. It was not a business for the faint of heart. It was a small business, and we needed every cent. For a man with no education, no land of his own, and a growing family to feed, business, no matter how small, was everything.

Before I was even a teenager, I was already part of this system, learning to scratch sisal just like my father. It was a tedious process that left my hands raw and sore, but in our family, you didn't wait until you were an adult to work. You worked as soon as you were old enough to hold a tool.

Cutting corners was never an option. While we knew others in the sisal business would leave their bundles out overnight to absorb dew and humidity, artificially increasing the weight, we were taught to run a clean business.

Naming Rights

There are so many stories from those early days of scratching sisal that still make me laugh unexpectedly. It was incredibly hard work, but we weren't just doing it for the money. The truth was, my father's real currency wasn't money, it was effort. He believed in work, in waking before the sun, in doing what had to be done, whether it paid off right away or not. He had no patience for laziness. Though life was often unfair, he never let us use that as an excuse. He raised us to believe we could control our effort, even if we couldn't control our circumstances.

I came into the world in 1984, but more than twenty years earlier, my dad was already walking through disasters that would reshape the course of his life. In the early days of October 1963, everything took a sharp turn and my family was caught in the middle of it.

That was the year Hurricane Flora, a Category 4 monster, tore through Haiti. When it hit Pianotte, it took everything in its path, including the house my father had built for his first wife and daughters. The wind howled, ripping at the weak cement walls and shaking the foundation until it was no longer safe to stay inside. As the roof peeled away and the house crumbled, my father grabbed Jeanitte, Yole, and whoever else was there, and they ran for their lives.

It wasn't until they were outside, breathless and soaked in rain, that someone realized the newborn was missing. Gougou, just days old, was still inside.

What followed was a scene too dramatic to fully capture in words. But this wasn't a story; it was my father's life. And it was my sister's beginning.

With the storm still raging, my father ran back inside, clawing through debris, tearing apart what remained of the house with his bare hands. Rain poured down. The wind howled. Still, he dug and dug, pulling at splintered wood and crumbling walls until he found her, alive. Miraculously alive. Buried beneath the wreckage.

But the storm had left its mark. Gougou survived, but she never spoke a word. She never heard a sound. To this day, she is deaf. No one knows whether it was the trauma of the hurricane, an accident, or something she was born with, but her silence became part of our family's story.

Yet despite her lack of speech, no one could ever say she wasn't brilliant. Gougou was and still is sharp as a blade. She may not hear, but she listens. She may not speak, but she communicates in ways that go far beyond words.

None of us in the Obrand family ever went to a deaf school, but somehow, we created our own way of talking to Gougou. She never attended school, yet she could tell a story from start to finish with such rich detail, more than words could ever capture. Sometimes, I wonder how we all just figured it out, our own little language with her.

Most of the signs we used were originals, made up by my dad and Gougou's two sisters. I spent hours observing and repeating until my hands could speak. Asking Gougou for water was as simple as mimicking drinking from a cup. If I needed juice, I'd gesture stirring an imaginary cup. Prayer was translated by the sign of the cross. Every gesture held meaning, and through them, we established a channel of communication that made sense to us as a family.

Gougou is also one of the best cooks in the family. Even though she doesn't hear or speak, you can tell right away if you've made her mad, it's almost instant. But she's also one of the best huggers I know. Every time I see her, her joyful sound is the best greeting I could ever ask for.

Six years after Flora, Jeanitte passed away in 1969 at the age of just 31. My father remarried, and my mother, Esther, became the new pillar of our growing family. If my father was a man of labor, my mother was a woman of faith.

She was devoted, so devoted that, if you looked closely, you might have seen a rosary bead pattern etched into her fingertips from years of prayer. St. Rose of Lima Catholic Church was her second home. And she didn't just attend Mass; she led services when the priest wasn't around. Not the sacraments, of course, she wasn't that Catholic, but when it came to prayers, funerals, and church gatherings, my mother was trusted as much as any ordained leader.

She lived and breathed Catholicism. She knew the church and its people like her own family. The nearly 25-minute walk from our home to church was never a barrier. In fact, there were days she made the trip twice, depending on what was going on.

Because of a shortage of priests in Haiti, many churches didn't have one permanently assigned. For more than four decades, St. Rose of Lima wasn't a parish; it was a chapel, a Catholic church without a priest. In the town where I grew up, we understood the difference. Occasionally, maybe once or twice a year, a visiting priest would come, but there were no guarantees. So, my mother was revered in the community for her service to the church. Everyone knew Sister Esther, or as they referred to her, *Soeur Esther.*

She started a prayer group before I was even born, and by the time I came into the world in 1984, it had already become an institution in Gris-Gris. These weren't casual gatherings. My mother, along with a few dozen of what we called the *Church Ladies*, didn't just pray the way most people pray. They had long, soul-deep conversations with God.

These women didn't pray while checking the time, wondering when dinner would be ready. No, they prayed through pain, through fear, through loss and poverty. If they needed to pray for twelve hours, they prayed for twelve hours. They prayed the sick back to health, money into the coffers, and food onto the table.

They moved heaven with those prayers. I often joke that my mother had Jesus on speed dial, because every time she prayed for something, an answer always followed. Whether it came as guidance, a solution, or sheer peace, something always came.

And we needed every prayer she could offer. Growing up, poverty wasn't an abstract concept. It was real. We knew we were poor because we felt it. Hunger wasn't subtle. It kicked the door down every morning, took a seat at the table, and shouted its name.

This was the dual mindset I was raised with: one where excuses didn't matter, only solutions, and the other, rooted deeply in God. My father found ways to feed us even when money was scarce. My mother found ways to deepen her faith even without formal education.

Yes, we went to bed hungry many nights. We missed school because we couldn't afford the fees. Life in Pianotte often felt like an uphill battle with no clear victory in sight. But still, my parents never let us believe we were defeated. I often wonder how my parents had the foresight to imagine a future for us when they were just fighting to survive from one day to the next. My father didn't own a single thing with his name on it, except for his birth certificate. No ID, no passport, not even a photo that I knew of. He never set foot in a bank or any other financial institution. Terms like life insurance, 401(k), or health insurance? They meant nothing to him. He lived in the present, day by day. And yet, somehow, he had a mindset always reaching toward a better tomorrow for his children.

It blows my mind every time I try to make sense of the balance between living for today and raising kids for a future that seemed so distant. My parents pushed education hard, relentlessly, honestly, sometimes to the point of annoyance. They made sure we all had a relationship with Jesus. Hard work and education were non-negotiable in our house.

They gave us something far more valuable than wealth. My father showed us the value of work. My mother showed us the power of faith. Together, they built something greater than money: They built resilience, determination, and the belief that a better tomorrow was always within reach. In a place where names carry weight, they gave us a legacy no title could ever match.

CHAPTER 2
Learning Without Letters

Growing up, my parents reminded us often that education was the key to success, but in a place like Gris-Gris, the door never seemed to fully open. It was always shut by a system where chaos and order fought for control.

In Gris-Gris, money spoke the loudest. It decided who got to go to school, who got fed, and it handed out futures like prizes, but only to a chosen few. I went to school not because we could afford it, but because my mother had a way of making things happen. With deep faith and sharp instincts, she knew how to bend the rules of poverty in our favor.

She was good friends with the principal of the local Catholic school, and that friendship became my ticket to a primary education. In first, second, and third grade, I sat in those classrooms dressed like the other children, but with no books, because we couldn't afford them. Still, somehow, I had a uniform. And what mattered most were the lessons I learned, lessons that would shape the rest of my life.

For my mother, sending us to school wasn't just about learning to read and write. School offered more than education; it offered a meal. When you grow up where we did, where food wasn't guaranteed and hunger was a daily threat, the promise of one meal a day was reason enough to find her children a seat in a classroom. One act. Two benefits. Education and nourishment, both essential, both life-changing.

For all her wisdom and strength, my mother couldn't read for most of my childhood. She had never set foot in a school, never sat at a desk, never spelled her own name on paper. But she knew the Bible better than anyone I'd ever met. Every verse, every story, every lesson lived inside her. She had memorized them all, passed down through sermons and prayer circles with the *Church Ladies*. But knowing the words and reading them are two different things.

When my mother led her prayer group, she gathered women so devoted they would wake at dawn, kneel for hours, and pray as if their words alone could shape the world. And then I would be called in to read the Bible aloud. I don't know how it started, but somehow, I became the designated *"Word*

19

Bringer." About thirty-five minutes into the morning prayers, the group would pause, and someone would ask, "Who will bring the word today?" They didn't wait for an answer, they already knew. My mother would glance at me, and I'd sigh, set aside whatever I was doing, and step forward with the Bible.

I did it for years, and for years my mother listened, absorbing the words she couldn't read herself. Then one day, at the age of fifty, she made the decision to learn.

"Imagine," she said, "if I could read the Bible on my own."

That was all the reason she needed. She enrolled in adult literacy classes, part of a government initiative under President Jean-Bertrand Aristide. Aristide, once a Catholic priest himself, had a vision for education that extended beyond children. He believed literacy should be possible for everyone, no matter their age. His campaign to eradicate illiteracy in Haiti during the mid to late 1990s gained widespread support with the slogan *'Analfabèt pa bèt'*, loosely translated as "Illiterates are not stupid." My mother took that message to heart.

She sat in a classroom, learning the letters she had only heard. She traced her fingers over the words she had spoken her whole life but had never truly seen. It took nearly twenty-four months of courage, and evening and weekend classes. But then it happened. She could read on her own. Her world got bigger and wider. She was only interested in reading one book.

Not novels. Not newspapers. Just one book. The only one that mattered: her Bible.

Reading was a central part of our family life, and having a book felt like holding buried treasure. We grew up without a television, without a radio, without even a clock to tell us when the day was done. I often joke that I grew up in the middle of nowhere, so remote that there was no TV (pun intended).

Time, for us, was measured in sunrises and sunsets, in the position of bright stars in the sky, in the sound of roosters announcing the morning, and the distant calls of mothers summoning their children home for the night.

I never saw a movie growing up. I never sat in front of a screen. Imagination was our television. Storytelling was our entertainment. And maybe that's why the Bible held such power in our household. It wasn't just words on a page, it was the only story we knew. And somehow, it was all we needed.

Then one day, someone from Port-au-Prince gifted us a crank radio, one of those old ones where you had to turn the handle for two minutes just to get ten minutes of sound. To us, it was a miracle.

That radio gave us access to two stations: Radio Lumière, a Christian network filled with sermons, prayers, and hymns, and Voice of America (VOA), a station that reported on the world beyond Haiti.

Without clocks in our house, the top-of-the-hour announcements on Radio Lumière became our way of telling time. It was such a simple thing, but knowing the time felt like power, a small grip on the larger world beyond our dusty roads.

When I think back on my childhood, I don't focus on the things we didn't have. I think about the ways we adapted: how my mother turned prayer into a daily ritual, how my father turned sisal into survival, and how a simple crank radio turned silence into connection.

We walked those dusty roads and lived by the rhythm of the sun, but what we carried home wasn't just an education. It was resilience. It was our story. And it was the deep belief that learning could open every door.

CHAPTER 3
Written in the
Margins

In Gris-Gris, time moved slow, and tradition never hurried. Life unfolded on its own terms, never asking for suggestions or permission. We had nothing against comfort or ease; they simply never came knocking on our door. Modern life was a stranger whose name we only knew from rumors. In our village, traditions and religious beliefs tangled themselves tightly together. Separating what was required from what was simply preferred felt like playing musical chairs.

I have witnessed firsthand the deep-rooted traditions that shape life in Haiti. Some of these customs make perfect sense, while others remain shrouded in mystery, passed down through generations without question or explanation. Many of these traditions still persist today as deeply embedded practices that reflect the ways Haitians have learned to navigate life.

Haiti is, and will likely remain, a country of contradictions. But it's also a place where survival and faith have always walked hand in hand, just as my parents taught their children to live. Still, nothing compares to the unbelievable stories and customs, the ones only God can explain, that are simply part of everyday life.

One custom I witnessed growing up was the reluctance of parents to name their children too early. In the U.S., expectant parents often spend months choosing the perfect name, sometimes even before pregnancy begins. Some throw gender reveal parties and celebrate the baby's identity long before birth.

In Haiti, things are different. Many babies, myself included, weren't named right away. It was common for parents to wait days or even weeks before deciding on a name. Why? Because infant mortality was a harsh reality. For generations, childbirth in Haiti was a fragile, uncertain event. Babies often didn't survive their first days or weeks, and mothers knew this all too well. Naming a child before there was confidence they would live was seen as premature. It felt like tempting fate and inviting heartbreak. It wasn't a lack of love. It was a lesson shaped by loss. Life was never guaranteed.

When a child had a name, the grief of losing them cut even deeper.

My mother, like many women in our town, gave birth at home, assisted by a midwife who had never set foot in a classroom but had safely delivered hundreds of babies. She knew which herbs to use, how to position a laboring mother, and how to bring a child into the world without the help of modern medicine. In our village, this kind of knowledge was passed down through generations. It was practical, life-saving, and completely outside the formal medical system.

The timing of naming a child was just one way history and culture shaped our lives. Another force, quieter, but just as powerful, was language. Haiti has two official languages: Haitian Creole and French. But the reality is far more complex.

Creole is the language of the people. Every Haitian speaks it, rich or poor, educated or not. It's the language of the streets, the markets, the homes, and the churches. It carries the voices of our parents, our ancestors, and our history. French, however, is the language of power, rooted in Haiti's colonial past. When the French colonized the country in the 18th century, they brought with them commerce, government, and control through crops such as coffee and sugarcane. French became the official language of law, politics, and business. It came to represent education and intelligence, even though only a small fraction of Haitians spoke it fluently. Speaking French well marked you as elite, superior, and more worthy of respect.

But make a mistake in French, and suddenly, you were seen as less educated, less capable, and less important. It's taken so seriously that some politicians have allegedly even lost elections over mispronouncing French words. That's how deep the divide goes.

France also brought slavery to Haiti, laying the foundation for what would become the first successful slave revolt in history. In 1804, Haiti emerged as the first Black nation to gain independence by overthrowing its colonizers. For a small Caribbean country to defeat a powerful European empire was no small feat. The pride of the people burned bright as they reclaimed their homeland from French oppression. Yet, the language of the oppressor remained.

When I was in school, Creole was forbidden in the classroom, even though both Creole and French were recognized languages. We could speak it during recess or after school with friends, but inside the classroom, only French was allowed. I grew up learning and studying mostly in French, memorizing instead of truly understanding.

Some of the French lessons I memorized back in fourth and fifth grade didn't make sense to me in Creole until after I'd graduated high school. I could recite them and ace any test, but the meaning was never really there. All those years as a student, memorization was behind the wheel and understanding hadn't even gotten in the car. Imagine trying to learn when the language of instruction isn't even the one you speak at home. That was, and still is, the reality for most Haitian students.

Growing up in Haiti, language has always been a question with no clear answer. Creole and French shared the title of "official," but we, as a nation, have never agreed on which should guide our future. Creole was, and still is, the language of the masses. It was developed and perfected by enslaved Africans who refused to be silent. Still, for much of our history, it was treated as less than. When Haiti shifted from dictatorship to democracy in 1987, we inserted Creole into the newly created constitution as an official language, but the shift in people's hearts was slow. French still fills pulpits and podiums, often more to impress than to connect. I had been to enough Haitian church services in French to know most people in the pews probably understood less than a quarter of what was being said.

Even with the linguistic ambivalence in the education system, going to school was a dream most parents had for their children. I never owned a single textbook. Throughout my entire elementary school education, from kindergarten through seventh grade, I didn't even have a backpack, because I had no books to carry. I survived by befriending classmates who had books, studying with them, borrowing pages when I could, and absorbing as much as possible through sheer determination.

Fortunately, in primary school, the subjects came easily to me. I didn't struggle much academically. Learning was challenging but in a fun, engaging way.

In a country where your name could be reshaped and your language silenced, surviving through creativity and persistence became its own kind of education. And somehow, without books or prestige, I was learning what mattered most.

CHAPTER 4
One God in a Land of Many

When my daughter was born, I gave her the only name that made sense to me: my mother's. That name meant faith, and faith is what raised me.

Throughout this book, I'll share more stories about my mother—her laughter, her grit, and her unwavering belief. She lived with open hands and an open heart, trusting God for everything and worrying about nothing.

Her faith was rooted in Catholicism, but her worship style and personal devotion resembled the kind of evangelical Christianity many Haitians later embraced. While some people in Haiti (and even in the U.S.) draw a faint line between the two, my mother embodied the best of both worlds.

Catholicism dominated Haitian culture throughout my childhood, but my mother constantly reminded us that religious affiliation mattered far less than living out your faith, being good to others, living a moral life, and placing your full trust in God.

In our town, your devotion to the church shaped how people saw you. But as evangelical Christianity began spreading in the early 1990s, Catholics were increasingly seen as less faithful, almost as if they needed saving. Critics often pointed to the practice of praying to statues or revering the Virgin Mary. Exodus 20:4–5 was frequently cited, those verses warning against making and worshiping graven images, stoking division within the faith itself.

"You shall not make for yourself an image in the form of anything in heaven above or on the earth beneath or in the waters below. You shall not bow down to them or worship them." **(Exodus 20:4–5, NIV).**

But my mother never got caught up in those debates. She kept her focus on the sovereignty of God.

Sovereignty. That word stayed with me growing up in Haiti. I first heard it in political conversations. Haiti stood proud in its independence as a symbol of freedom. Time and again, I heard the phrase, "Haiti is a sovereign nation," especially whenever foreign powers tried to interfere in our internal affairs. That's how I first understood sovereignty: as bold independence.

Then one day, a missionary on Radio Lumière spoke about God's sovereignty. That was something new in a divine context. What did it mean for God to be sovereign? Was it about power? About control? About leadership? It was a word that felt real but distant, like something I could sense but not quite grasp. Then life started showing me. My mother's quiet strength, the way she trusted God with everything, was a textbook example of God's sovereignty. That's when I began to understand what the word truly meant. Listening to sermons on the radio widened my worldview and deepened my faith.

I had grown up hearing only Catholic sermons and traditional Haitian preaching, where heaven was always described as the place where pain and suffering came to an end. That was the version of heaven I held on to, a place of rest, of relief. But then came the voices of foreign missionaries on the radio. They spoke of heaven in a way I hadn't heard before. They painted it with streets of gold and walls made of precious stones, like something out of a dream. They quoted Revelation chapter 21, describing a New Jerusalem overflowing with light, glory, and abundance.

It was beautiful, but it was also foreign. The idea of abundance, of gold-lined streets and endless beauty, didn't quite fit into my everyday world. Where we lived, poverty wasn't the backdrop; it was center stage. For us, imagining heaven as anything more than the absence of suffering already felt like hope enough. Luxury was a language we didn't speak.

Still, I listened. And little by little my understanding of heaven began to widen, not to replace the version I had always known, but to hold both truths: that heaven is both a place of peace and a place of unimaginable beauty. That for those of us who knew lack, even the absence of pain is abundance.

My family was deeply involved in church life. My mom was a spiritual powerhouse, known throughout the village as a woman who walked hand in hand with Jesus. She wasn't the kind of believer who just went to church; she lived her faith. Her prayers would ring out long after the rest of us had fallen asleep. If you passed by our home after sundown, you might hear her whispering scripture or calling out to God in prayer. For her, faith wasn't reserved for Sundays, it was a daily necessity.

Sunday wasn't special; it was just another day to worship. My siblings and I were all active in church as well. I used to read scripture during Mass at St. Rose of Lima in Gris-Gris. Later, after I moved to Port-au-Prince, I served as an altar boy at St. Anne's, near downtown. I served both the five a.m. weekday services and the nine a.m. Sunday Masses.

But the sovereignty of God never came up in those sacred spaces where you'd expect to hear it. In later years, I began hearing preachers and missionaries speak about God's sovereignty. But by then, I had already formed my understanding from the things my mother endured without ever complaining. That was the beginning of the paradigm shift. It was becoming clear that national sovereignty and divine sovereignty might ride the same train, but they were headed for different destinations.

The sovereignty my mother relied on had nothing to do with earthly governments, but rather from a supernatural power. Here was a woman more devoted than anyone I'd ever known, yet she struggled constantly. Every night, we lit kerosene lamps to study and warmed bathwater in a plastic jug left in the sun. There was no electricity. No running water. Sometimes, no food at all. My mother prayed to the God of heaven every single day, and still, the struggles remained. Why?

This was one of the first deep questions I wrestled with as a believer: Why do those who love God the most often suffer the most? But my mother's life taught me two things: Suffering is not reserved for unbelievers, and God's sovereignty means trusting Him even when we don't understand His ways.

Many others didn't share my mother's perspective. They expected something from God; they weren't content with the privilege of simply worshiping Him. So when God didn't meet their expectations, they looked elsewhere to have their needs met. And the culture was ready and willing to offer an alternative: voodoo.

In Haiti, there's a saying: "Haiti is eighty percent Catholic and ninety-five percent voodoo." It might sound like a joke, but it reveals a truth that shapes much of the country's spiritual reality. Even those who identify as Christians often participate in rituals meant to "keep the spirits happy." They believe in God, but they also fear the spirits, so they appease them just in case.

If a child got sick, it wasn't uncommon to hear someone say, "Before going to the hospital, you should visit the voodoo priest to make sure nothing spiritual is going on." Even among those who wouldn't call themselves voodoo practitioners, many still honored their ancestors or performed small rituals, lighting a candle, burning certain herbs, avoiding particular phrases. All done out of caution, to avoid offending the spirits.

But not in my house.

My mom didn't play around with that. There was no gray area, no halfway. It was God or nothing. She didn't fear the spirits. She didn't acknowledge them. She used to say, "They have no place in my house, and they will have no place in my life." In a country where most people believed in both God and spirits, my mom believed in only one: the Sovereign God.

Are you sick? Talk to God before you talk to a doctor. It wasn't that my mom rejected modern medicine, she just chose to live with a faith-first mindset. Are you hungry? Talk to God. Are you hurting deep inside? Talk to God. Whether the days were easy, heavy, or somewhere in between, her answer never changed: talk to God. Her unwavering faith made me confront my own beliefs. Did I believe God was truly in control? Did I believe He had power over the spirits people feared? Over the sicknesses we endured? Over the poverty we lived through?

Through watching her life, her suffering, and her unwavering consistency, I learned something: Sovereignty doesn't mean your life is easy; it means God reigns even when things don't make sense. It means He has a plan that's bigger than your moment of pain, bigger than voodoo, bigger than poverty, bigger than loss.

It means He is still God, even when the world is falling apart. I believe this not just because I read it but because I saw it in her life, in her prayers, in her suffering, in her strength, and in her steadfast devotion. In a land of many gods, she taught me there is only one worth trusting.

Through her, I came to understand that sovereignty isn't about removing pain; it's about trusting the One who reigns through it.

CHAPTER 5
The Weight We Carried

There were no scales in our house, except the one my dad used to weigh sisal. In a place where most things were measured by estimation, people rarely complained about the weight of their cross. In Gris-Gris, life didn't check your age before handing you a burden. Willing or not, you carried what you were given. And for me, it started with carrying water.

The sun wasn't kind in the early morning, yet we still walked an hour each way just to fetch water before we could drink, cook, or bathe. That was life.

The rules in our house were non-negotiable. My parents, though they had never been to school themselves, made it clear that education came first. No matter how tired we were or how hot it got, we had to finish our homework as soon as we got home.

The second rule was just as important: fetch the water. In Pianotte, there was no running water, no faucets to turn on, and no pipes hidden behind the walls. Water was something we had to go and get. And getting it was no small task.

Every day before and after school, my siblings and I walked an hour each way to fetch water, carrying either large jugs or five-gallon buckets back home. On some days when the sun was especially brutal, the walk felt twice as long. The road wasn't paved or smooth; it was a winding, dusty path scattered with rocks and thorns, rising and dipping through the landscape.

The first time I was old enough to carry my own full jug, I thought I was being punished. My arms felt like they were being yanked from their sockets, my legs trembled under the weight, and every step made the journey feel impossible. Unfortunately, the hardest stretch, the part where I had to carry the full jug uphill, always came near the end.

But the thing about life in Haiti is that difficulty isn't an excuse. The water had to be fetched, and that was that. The water source wasn't a well; it was a natural spring—a small opening in the earth where water pooled just enough for us to collect it. After heavy rains the water sometimes turned muddy, and we'd have to wait for it to settle before filling our buckets.

Fetching water was also a social event. Everyone in the village—children, women, and even some of the older men — gathered there. We often timed our trips to meet up with neighbors so we could walk together, trading stories and laughter to make the tough journey feel lighter. That's when I began to understand that fetching water wasn't just about drinking, washing, or cooking; it was also about connection. People shared news, gossiped, laughed, and sometimes argued. The walk to the spring was quiet and wearying, but once we arrived, exhaustion gave way to community.

There was an unspoken order at the spring: Older women always went first. The rest of us, especially the kids, had to wait our turn. There was no rushing the process. Cutting the line would earn you a sharp scolding or, worse, send you straight to the back. When it was finally our turn, we squatted by the water, dipped our buckets in carefully, and tried not to stir up the dirt. One wrong move, and you'd end up hauling back a bucket full of muddy water. No one wanted mud in their dinner or worse, to drink water mixed with sand or other uninvited guests.

The walk to water was tiring, but the walk back home was something else entirely. Five gallons of water weighs around forty pounds, and when you're a kid that might as well be the weight of the world. I started with just one gallon, but before I turned eight my load had doubled to two. My sisters were experts, carrying five-gallon buckets on their heads without using their hands. That technique took serious strength and perfect posture.

Others carried full buckets in their hands, switching from one arm to the other every few minutes when the pain became too much. By the time we reached home, our clothes were usually soaked with sweat, our shoulders ached, and our hands were stiff from gripping the rough plastic edges of the buckets or our yellow jugs. But no one praised us. No one clapped. Just another chore. Just another day.

Bringing water home wasn't seen as a victory; it was just survival. We didn't have an endless supply. Every drop mattered because once it ran out, someone had to make the trip all over again. Water was power, and in a place where nothing came easy, power was something worth fighting for.

As I got older, the journey became second nature. My body adjusted, my hands grew calloused, and my legs grew stronger. Sometimes, my siblings and I made an extra trip just to bathe in the river. My older brother taught us that trick; one less person to wash at home meant a little less water used.

Over time, fetching water didn't feel so heavy unless we were hungry. Eventually, I stopped seeing the walk as something to complain about. It became part of growing up, a way we learned resilience and what it meant to carry something for the good of others. That lesson stayed with me long after I left Pianotte.

The Weight We Carried

Where we lived water wasn't just heavy, it was like gold.
And we brought it back, one sore footstep at a time.

CHAPTER 6
Problems Never End

In Haiti, we have a saying that rolls off the tongue almost like a sigh: *Pwoblèm pap janm fini* (problems never end). People say it after bad news, during hard times, or sometimes just while shaking their heads over a flat tire, or when one problem shows up just as they're closing the book on another.

It's not dramatic. It's just the truth, spoken plainly. Another way we put it is: *Dèyè mòn gen mòn* (behind one mountain, there's always another). I heard that a lot growing up in the Obrand household. At first it sounded like something adults said to fill the silence. But the older I got, the more I began to feel its weight. It wasn't just about struggle. It was

41

about the way life keeps going, one challenge folding into the next.

That idea has stayed with me, shaped me and in some ways, steadied me. In the stories ahead—moments pulled from real days, real choices—I came to understand those words in a deeper way. Sometimes painfully. Sometimes with unexpected grace.

Growing up, all of my siblings lived under the same roof in Gris-Gris. Our family was close-knit. For years, we were rarely apart, even for short periods of time. An overnight stay-away was almost unheard of. But as the new millennium began, change slowly crept into our town. Not loud or disruptive change, just the kind that quietly reshaped everyday life for my family.

In the late 1990s, a group of missionaries from Minnesota began visiting our community. It was the first time I saw white people in our village. At first, they were just a few unfamiliar faces at Sunday Mass. They smiled politely, nodded along to the hymns, and did their best to follow the rhythm of a place so far from their own.

They came through the Parish Twinning of America, a program that connects churches in the U.S. with parishes in Haiti, usually small, often overlooked ones, where a little bit of support can go a long way.

Somehow, maybe by chance, maybe by grace, our little church, St. Rose of Lima, was chosen to be partnered with theirs: Church of the Risen Savior, based in Burnsville, Minnesota.

Their arrival was transformative. They began with the rehabilitation and expansion of our church, St. Rose of Lima. When they came, the original building could barely hold 150 people. With their help, a new church was built, one that could seat well over 1,000. Not long after, they helped expand St. Rose of Lima School, giving students a modern learning space. This solved a major problem in our community. But many more remained beyond the church and school walls.

Perhaps their most important project addressed the issue of water. When they saw the process of fetching it, they were moved. They couldn't understand how, in this day and age, Gris-Grisians had to walk more than an hour to collect water that wasn't even safe to drink. They were stunned. Something had to be done.

The missionaries wanted to drill water wells. We were overjoyed. For most of our lives, we walked more than sixty minutes each way to collect what we believed was clean water. So when the drilling crew arrived, they got to work and drilled several wells. One of them was built less than a hundred yards from our house.

It was revolutionary. A game changer. But with this new convenience came a lesson. When the water was far away, we were disciplined. We fetched it every evening so we'd never be without, especially at night. But now, with water so close by, we started to take it for granted. There were many mornings we woke up to find no water in the house, even though it was just steps away. It taught us that even blessings can be mismanaged. That hardship breeds discipline.

As the rhythms of daily life shaped us, the lives around us left their mark too. Living where we did, and living how we did, meant that tragedies hit hard and unexpected. We knew everyone in the village and they knew us. Their pain was our pain. Their joys, our joys. So when my brother Claudy suddenly disappeared in 2002, it rocked our community as much as it rocked our family.

He was the fifth of ten siblings and had never left Gris-Gris. At twenty-four, Claudy showed no signs of preparing for a sudden journey, yet one morning, he vanished without a trace. Some of his clothes were missing, though not all. It looked deliberate, but no one knew where he had gone or why.

In Haiti, we use radio stations to spread the word about missing persons. But airtime is expensive, and we didn't have the money. Days turned into weeks. Then months. Our grief was inconsolable. People began telling my mother they had dreamed about him. Some claimed he was dead and buried.

We feared the worst.

Some even suggested we consult a voodoo priest. They said such people could see what we couldn't. But we refused. During those hard and uncertain days, I watched my mother's faith hold firm. Even if it was only the size of a mustard seed, her prayers had the power to cause mountains to shake. Each passing week seemed to deepen her resolve. Her eyes stayed locked on the hope of finding answers about the whereabouts of her second-born son. When weeks turned into months and months rolled into a year, her prayers raced as if they could outrun doubt itself. When His answers didn't come, she didn't back down, if anything, she pressed on. *"Well God, you started this. Now it's yours to finish."*

Then, nearly 18 months later, as suddenly as he had vanished, Claudy returned. He had been living in the Dominican Republic, working in a batey, a settlement for undocumented Haitian laborers cutting sugarcane. He left without telling anyone because he wanted to experience life beyond our village and didn't want to be talked out of it. But he got more than he bargained for. He endured brutal working conditions, earning just twenty U.S. dollars a month, barely enough to live on. Despite our anger, we welcomed him home. He returned with nothing but the clothes on his back and a Dominican rooster meant for cockfighting.

We were furious.

We were relieved.

We were confused.

A storm of emotions stirred inside us as a family. We didn't call it grace when we welcomed my brother back, but grace filled the house in quiet and steady ways. As the Word

45

Bringer of the family, I couldn't help but see Claudy's return as our own version of the Prodigal Son, a biblical story I had read to my mother more times than I could count (Luke 15:11–32). In that parable, the son returns home after wasting his inheritance and his father welcomed him with open arms. Except in our version Claudy didn't leave with a pile of money, and he didn't come home to a house with much either. But he returned to a place where grace and forgiveness flowed freely, like water from a spring.

Meanwhile, life in Gris-Gris moved at its gentle pace, unaware of the gap Claudy had left behind. The missionary group continued their work, tackling problems we had learned to navigate for generations. Then came a new project for our village: the construction of a bakery.

Haitians love bread, and my siblings and I were no exception. The new bakery introduced modern ovens, propane fuel, and ingredients like milk and sugar. My brothers, Joel, Claudy, and Tinel, were hired there.

Then one day, Claudy, the brother who had once disappeared without a trace, was caught in a terrible accident. He had been working with an electric dough roller. While he was cleaning it, someone accidentally switched it on. His right hand was trapped between two thick steel rollers.

Bones cracked under pressure. Bits of bone flew, striking the tin roof with the soft, scattered sound of sand blowing in a storm. Joel rushed home on a motorcycle, breathing hard, his face pale and shaken. He didn't say a word, but we could already tell, something had gone terribly wrong.

"Shoot. Shoot. We have a problem. Hey, I need a couple of us to run with Claudy. His hand is flattened." We had no time to ask questions or feel our fear. The nearest hospital was hours away. All that mattered now was getting Claudy there in time.

Problems never end.

Claudy rode four hours by motorcycle to reach the hospital in Les Cayes, his hand crushed, his body screaming in pain. Gris-Gris had no hospital, just bumpy gravel roads and community prayers.

That day, the journey reminded us how closely life and hardship walk together. Every bump in the road stretched time. Still, it was the fastest ride of his life. We had no money for the hospital, but pain has a way of reordering priorities. Stopping it came first.

Claudy spent 21 days in the hospital as doctors worked to rebuild his hand. Months and years later, the damage is visible, the scars, the hollowed-out valleys that mark where bone and flesh once held strong.

The hospital bill was overwhelming, and we saw no clear way to pay it. But our community came together, the church, the bakery, our neighbors. Together, we made sure Claudy got home, and we tackled the remaining balance. That's what we mean when we say problems never end. Behind every solution waits another challenge.

But just as problems never end, neither does the grace that carries us through. Behind every mountain, another rises, but so does the strength to climb.

CHAPTER 7
Raised by Many— Fed by a Few

In Gris-Gris, respect was the ticket. Obedience was the bouncer. You couldn't get far without both. It didn't matter what your last name was or who your parents were. Those two ruled the place, and every kid learned the system as soon as they were old enough to take their first steps.

Haitian culture valued community discipline, sometimes to an extreme. In many Haitian homes, parenting was a split system: part compassion, part control. Ours was no different.

In my house, I grew up under two very different styles of leadership. If our family had been a country, it would've had a dual government, part democracy, part dictatorship. My mother ran things like a democratic leader: negotiating, listening, offering second chances, and occasionally bending the rules in the name of mercy.

My father, on the other hand, was a dictator through and through. He ruled with few words but absolute authority. When he made a decision, there was no appeal process. For my dad, a two-minute warning wasn't a thing. Obedience was a prerequisite. He didn't believe in long speeches or drawn-out explanations. He was all about order, discipline, and consequences.

If he walked into a room and saw something out of place, he didn't need to ask who was responsible. He simply gave a look and we knew what was expected. If we failed to meet those expectations, there were no discussions or debates. Just discipline.

On one hand, you knew there'd be consequences for breaking the rules. On the other hand, you never quite knew what form those consequences would take. Kneeling for what felt like hours was always a possibility. Sometimes, it meant grabbing your right ear like a steering wheel and driving you to a quiet corner to "have a word" about your misdeeds. My father didn't yell. He didn't repeat himself. He didn't argue. He spoke once, and that was the law. Most of my whoopings came from my father. In Haiti, corporal punishment wasn't just accepted, it was expected. My father didn't hit out of anger or frustration; it was simply how discipline was enforced.

My father wasn't cruel. He was as firm as firm could be. He used discipline to correct troubled behaviors he saw in us, knowing they could lead to bigger problems later in life. For a man of few words, each word he spoke mattered. One piece of advice he repeated often was, *"Mache sou 13 men pa pile 14,"* loosely translated as "Walk on 13, but do not dare 14." It's a proverbial caution, like walking a tightrope. For my dad, it meant we should live carefully, act cautiously, and never overstep the boundaries he set. It is a lesson that has served me well to this day.

When he disciplined us, he was methodical. If you did something wrong, he would wait, not out of mercy, but to ensure that when punishment came it was delivered calmly, deliberately, and without emotion. That was his way.

Thankfully, my mother was often the safeguard between us and his iron fist. Where my father was the law, my mother was the public defender. She pleaded our cases and found loopholes in the system that often softened his judgments, stepping in at just the right moment to say, "Okay, that's enough."

There were times when, instead of corporal punishment, I'd be tasked with making two or three trips to fetch water in a single day. These "deals" were often negotiated by my mother, almost like two governments hashing out an international trade agreement.

Of course, my mother was no pushover. She had her own ways of enforcing discipline, but they were very different from my father's. She believed in lectures, prayers, guilt trips, and emotional lessons rather than physical punishment. Sometimes, her punishments lasted longer than my father's because they targeted the mind instead of the body. Where my father's whooping lasted a few minutes, my mother's moral lessons could stretch on for hours or even days.

She sat us down and talked, telling us stories about God, about consequences, about how our actions would shape our future. She had a way of making you feel so guilty that, by the time she finished, I sometimes wished she had just whooped me and been done with it. I was always amazed by some of the words my mother used in conversation. Despite never having received a formal education, I often wondered where she learned those big words, many of them in French, that even we kids who actually went to school didn't know.

Despite their different styles, my parents shared one core rule: Respect was non-negotiable.

In our village, that rule extended far beyond our household. It was common for the Obrand kids to refer to elderly members of the community as "Mom" or "Auntie" even if they weren't related to us by blood.

One of the most confusing aspects of my childhood, something that still lingers in my mind today, was how any adult could discipline us. In Pianotte, parenting was a community effort. If an adult saw us doing something wrong, it didn't matter whether they were related or not. Any "Mom" or "Auntie" had the right to step in and correct us on the spot. And by correct, I don't mean a stern talking-to. I mean they could whoop us right there in public. No questions asked.

If an elder saw a child being disrespectful or acting out, they could grab them, discipline them, and not a single parent would object. Then when we got home, our parents would whoop us again just for good measure.

I remember once getting caught by a neighbor while playing near a field we weren't supposed to be in. He wasn't even a close family friend, but he called me over, spanked me for what felt like several minutes, and told me to head home.

When I got there, my father asked where I had been. I told him, expecting him to be upset with the neighbor. Instead, he said, "Good. That means you won't do it again."

At the time, I couldn't understand how someone outside my family had that kind of authority. But now I see it clearly. It was protection, but it was also pressure. Being raised by everyone meant being accountable to everyone.

In Haiti, discipline wasn't just about punishment. It was about upholding community values. But here's where things got strange: Anyone could whoop us, but no one could feed us. As much as our village operated on shared discipline, it had strict rules when it came to trusting others with food.

My parents' number one rule in this area was: "Do not eat from anyone." We were taught from a young age that taking food from neighbors was dangerous. In the United States, kids are taught about "stranger danger" at an early age, but that concept doesn't quite exist in Haiti. Or at least, it exists in a very different context.

There's a deep sense of community among village residents. We pray together, and when there's a death in a family, we all feel it as if we were one. But if my house were a government, then when it came to food, going to a neighbor's house for a meal wasn't just a minor infraction —it was more like committing a felony, not because of hygiene or allergies, but because of voodoo and poisoning. There were too many stories of children who had eaten a piece of candy or a plate of food from the wrong person and died inexplicably hours later. Whispers would spread through the village:

"Maybe they ate something from so-and-so."

"Maybe someone put a curse in their food."

"Maybe one of the neighbors is an undercover witch doctor who fed them a certain kind of food, killed them, and turned them into a zombie."

Like most things in life, even the strictest rules make room for exceptions. There was one day a year when eating at someone else's house wasn't just allowed, but necessary: January 1st, our Independence Day. This day wasn't just a date on the calendar; it carried history and pride. At the center of it all was soup. Not just any soup, pumpkin soup, widely known across the country as *freedom soup*.

Before Haiti became independent in 1804, only the French colonizers got to enjoy pumpkin soup. It was seen as a delicacy, too good for the enslaved. But once Haiti gained its independence, we flipped the script. We made that very same dish the symbol of our freedom.

In Pianotte, bowls of hot pumpkin soup traveled from house to house. Our family had our route. Neighbors waited with their pots and hungry smiles, eager to taste ours. And we waited just as eagerly for theirs. In some ways, January 1st felt like Haiti's own kind of Thanksgiving holiday. It was joyful. It was sacred. But once the sun rose on January 2nd, the old rule slid quietly back into place. We didn't eat from anyone. Even leftover soup would be a violation of the rules.

Fear of witchcraft and poison ran so high that eating at anyone's house, even a close friend, was strictly off the table. You're probably wondering why my mom, with her unshakable faith in God, still played by these unwritten community food rules. Well, in Pianotte, believing in God and honoring tradition felt like two drivers on the same road. Whereas faith carried insurance, tradition was in and out of its lane, without a license, both speeding up and down the highway of life.

If we got sick, extreme measures were used to get us well again. I still don't know how we made it through some of the practices we survived. But somehow, we did.

When my brother Tinel fell thirty feet from a coconut tree, my mother's first instinct was to pour a glass of kerosene and make him drink it. For weeks, his burps were painfully uncomfortable; every time he burped, it was pure kerosene.

There were other unusual remedies, too. If I had a deep cut, ashes from burnt wood were rubbed into the wound. If a child had asthma, they were tricked into drinking a glass of milk with a dead mouse hidden inside, the idea being that the shock would cure them. It wasn't unusual to see adults or children sniffing moonshine or rubbing alcohol, believing it could alleviate a headache. For those who suffered from motion sickness, it wasn't uncommon to suggest they lick the dirty tires of the truck before getting in. I've personally witnessed this more times than I can count.

These remedies may sound strange, even dangerous, but they were deeply embedded in our culture. And despite it all, we survived. Haiti remains a place where tradition and modernity, faith and superstition, hardship and resilience coexist. Growing up in Pianotte meant navigating those contradictions daily. Some made sense. Others confused me. But all of them, somehow, still live in me today.

We lived lives that were both deeply communal and deeply mysterious. Often, the line between survival and faith was blurred. Despite having no money, no security, and no guarantees, my parents still believed that education and faith could change everything.

PART TWO

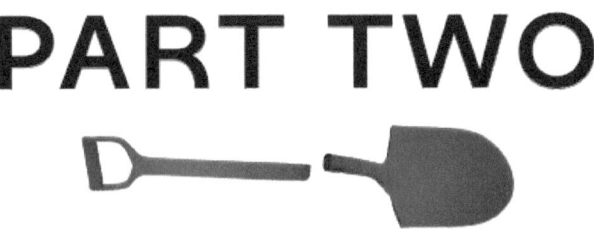

CHAPTER 8
Compelled to Appear

My mom was known throughout Gris-Gris as someone with a VIP pass to Jesus. If there was a spiritual crisis, a dark presence, or someone in need of healing prayer, people knew exactly where to turn. Her reputation wasn't limited to our neighborhood, folks from nearby towns came too.

Her feats were legendary, both to outsiders and to her own children. We thought she was amazing. I watched her chase evil spirits out of people and do things most only read about in the Old Testament. She stood firm against spiritual forces that left the rest of us shaking, performing all kinds of miracles, just shy of walking on water or raising the dead.

When the Bible said, "All things are possible," she believed it with every fiber of her being. That's why she could move heaven and earth.

In certain developed nations like the United States, many Christians treat stories in the Bible about spiritual warfare and miracles as historical accounts, things that happened long ago. But in Haiti, especially where I grew up, those things weren't just in the past. They were real. They happened all the time.

The devil my mother battled was smarter than most people gave him credit for. In Haiti, where poverty ran deep and physical suffering was everywhere, the enemy used different distractions than he did in places of wealth. He used addiction to cheap alcohol like moonshine, obsession with the lottery, and other cultural vices that destroyed lives and tore families apart. I watched it eat away at many of my relatives' happiness until there was nothing left but poverty and despair. They gambled their lives away for a one-in-a-billion chance.

My mother stayed spiritually alert. She didn't just pray casually; she prayed with the authority of someone who knew God personally. At times, I'd hear my mom talking to God in a raised voice, like two friends arguing over how a TV show should've ended. No anger in her tone, just the sound of two people who are deeply convinced they saw things differently.

Several times a year, she and her circle of *Church Ladies* hosted what they called "6-to-6" gathering: praying nonstop from six a.m. to six p.m. No water. No food. Just prayer. And when they prayed, things happened. These women, who might have seemed powerless to the world, were some of the most powerful people in town.

Two moments involving my mother changed my understanding of faith forever.

The first happened one night as I was walking home from a friend's house and stepped on something strange. I was barefoot, we couldn't afford shoes. What I stepped on was a dried herring, lying in the middle of a path, miles from the ocean. We never figured out how it got there, six miles inland, or why the village dogs hadn't eaten it. That part remained a mystery. It pierced my right foot, and the pain was unbearable. Within a day, my foot swelled. I couldn't walk. I couldn't play. And that meant no soccer.

In Haiti, soccer was life. We didn't even have real balls—we used whatever we could find, even rolled-up banana leaves inside an old sock. Being stuck in bed would've hurt more than just my foot. So I didn't tell anyone, not even my siblings.

When my mother came home from prayer, she took one look at me and said, "You stepped on something weird, didn't you?" I had no idea how she could've known, but somehow, she knew. She prayed over me for at least an hour. By dinnertime, the swelling was completely gone. I was back on my feet like nothing had happened. That was the moment something shifted in my understanding of spiritual warfare.

I didn't think the herring ended up in the street was an accident. I believed it was a voodoo trap meant to harm someone. Maybe something had been placed on that fish to infect whoever stepped on it. Sadly, I was the one who found it. My mother's prayers saved my foot. But she never took credit; she gave all the glory to her Lord, Jesus Christ.

Some of you might be tempted to believe the darkness my mother battled only lives in faraway places like Haiti. But don't be fooled. The devil doesn't respect borders. He needs no visa. He shows up wherever he pleases, dressed for the culture he's invading. In Haiti and other poor countries where even food is seen as a luxury, he's loud. He uses hunger, desperation, and fear as his primary tactics.

In wealthier nations, where the measure of success is often thick bank accounts and large homes in gated neighborhoods, the devil works differently. He doesn't roar, he whispers. He doesn't tempt with food for the stomach, but with the shimmer of fame for the heart.

In Haiti, where more than half the population is unemployed, the devil doesn't have to try too hard. He plants his lies in the stillness, using idleness as fertile soil for his schemes. In wealthy nations in the West, the devil hums through extremely tight schedules. He doesn't need to scare you; he simply needs to keep you busy. Caught up. Pulled in a hundred directions. Wishing for twenty-five hours in a day. If he can keep you distracted, it might not be a win, but he has the ball. And the devil's greatest play is convincing you there's no battle at all. If you've started to believe that, your fire might already be getting cold. The fight is just as real in poor countries like Haiti as in developed nations like the United States. It's simply harder to notice in places where clocks and calendars are synchronized.

After my foot was healed, I went right back to playing soccer. I thought the herring incident had taught me all I needed to know about spiritual power. But a few years later, something else would happen that made the herring feel like a warning shot.

A man from our village who had built a successful life in France came back to visit. Most people who left Gris-Gris never returned, so we were honored to have him. He was someone my mother had helped raise.

He visited every few years, always parking his rental car in our yard before walking home. We were mesmerized by the car. He was kind and generous. He loved my mother and often gave her money to help with expenses. On this particular trip, he stayed for a month, two weeks longer than usual, and announced a massive feast to thank the spirits who had helped him succeed. Not just any spirits, but voodoo spirits.

He wanted my mother to be there. He said her presence would please the spirits. He often told people, "I owe a debt of gratitude to two people: the woman who helped raise me, and the spirits who give me wealth." He went on and on about the ceremony, saying he had hired a voodoo priest from Léogâne and tables of food would be spread from end to end. People from all over Haiti were coming to honor the spirits.

My mom cut him off before he could finish. "If it's a Thanksgiving Mass, I'll be there. But if it's a voodoo ceremony, I'll stay home. Never forget, the earth is the Lord's, and everything in it."

That didn't sit well with him. Like many who practiced voodoo, he'd say, "I have respect for those I do not see." But my mom served Jesus and wanted no part in the ceremony. She suggested he make it a Thanksgiving Mass instead.

"Nope."

Still, the rumors swirled. Word spread that our family was involved. Some even claimed we were organizing it. It wasn't true, but once the story got out, people believed it. Even some Catholic leaders did.

Then came the night of the ceremony. Though our mother had forbidden us to attend, my brothers and I secretly made a plan. In Haiti, if you planned a party for 500 people, a few thousand might show up. Word of free food and a real voodoo priest spread fast.

Motorcycles. Cars. People herding goats and chickens. It looked more like a festival than a ceremony. We snuck out and walked the thirty or forty minutes to the site. The moon lit the way. People were pouring in, some for the ritual, some for the feast. We couldn't miss it. But we had another reason. We feared the voodoo priest might force our mother to appear. That thought haunted us.

You might wonder how a voodoo priest could compel someone to show up at a ritual she wanted no part of. But trust me, I had seen firsthand what the dark power of voodoo could do. Voodoo had a way of bending reason and twisting what seemed impossible into reality. This ritual, we knew, could be a defining moment for us as a family. Could the spirits summon my mother and pull her into their circle? Could her prayers stand like a wall against any curse? We were about to find out.

Everyone there knew who we were. Ninety-five percent of the attendees referred to us as the children of Accevil and Esther. We just hoped our presence wouldn't make things worse. But we had to be there, not as participants, but as spectators.

We arrived, and within minutes the voodoo priest took his place. Purple robe. Red bandana. Sword in one hand, book in the other. Under the full moon and firelight, the rituals began. He chewed razor blades as if they were potato chips. He swallowed raw eggs like coconut water. He killed a chicken and drank its blood in a slow, deliberate manner to show his raw power. The crowd screamed. We could barely breathe.

Then something strange happened.

The priest stopped and asked the drummers to pause. "Hang on, something is off. Someone is interfering."

After a few minutes, he tried again but stopped a second time. For over ninety minutes, the ceremony started and stopped, over and over, like a DJ missing a key piece of equipment for his performance. Normally, the spirits possess the voodoo priest first, then a few people in the crowd. That's the sign they've arrived. But this party was stuck. People were confused.

The man from France said, "I think I know who's blocking this. Whatever we do, she's undoing." I panicked. I knew who he was referring to. I'd seen her praying before we left. What if they forced her to come? My heart pounded so loud it echoed in my ears. My thoughts slowed, like an old computer overloaded with too many tabs open. Everything blurred. A flood of questions crashed into me.

What if she came and the spirits struck her down?

What if her prayers weren't enough this time?

These weren't just worries. They felt like knives pressing into my chest. The organizer sent someone on a motorcycle to our house. We debated whether to run back and find out what they wanted. We couldn't decide. After all, the ceremony hadn't officially started. We decided to stay. All eyes were on the Obrand boys. If our mom was really interfering with such a well-planned and powerful ceremony and if she stood her ground, was there even the slightest chance they'd swap her for one of her children? In the world of voodoo, anything is possible, and the unexpected is almost certain.

When the messenger arrived at our house, my mom was exactly where we'd left her, Bible in one hand, rosary in the other. They reportedly asked her to stop praying. She agreed, but with one condition:

"Keep my name out of it."

As soon as the messenger returned, people got curious. What now? The circle of people got tighter. The crowd grew. The voodoo priest looked tense. "Someone was blocking the spirits to prove a point." He said with a firm tone. We knew who he meant.

Before the drumming could resume, the organizer stepped forward. In a short speech that blended Creole with fancy French, he said:

"Thank you all for coming to support this very important assembly and thank you for your patience. I had invited someone special tonight—the woman who raised me, Esther. But whatever we're trying to tie, she's untying. Whatever we're building, she's breaking. She's undoing it all."

The crowd reacted with a mix of boos and cheers. Someone shouted from deep in the crowd:

"Compel her to come here! Send the spirits to force her to show up right here!" The priest's facial expression changed. Jaw clenched. He tugged at his collar as his eyes scanned the crowd.

"No. We asked for permission instead. She is serving her God. We are serving our god. They are different."

Some of my siblings wanted to go home, but others were eager to see more. Was that really the end? Who had won the match? Was it my mom or the voodoo priest? I wasn't ready to roll the dice and leave. The night was charged with tension. Going home wouldn't mean sleep anyway. None of us were ready for that, so we decided to stay for a bit longer.

Within minutes, the voodoo priest gave a nod to his drummers and the ritual resumed. This time the shift was visible. The spirits arrived. People began to convulse. The drums pounded. The air grew heavy. The ceremony had finally begun.

That was the moment everything clicked for me. That's when I understood the power of prayer. Word spread quickly: Esther had blocked a voodoo ceremony. Some were amazed. Others were terrified. Later, we found out my mom hadn't prayed alone; she had called her prayer circle. Together, they stood their ground. It wasn't just my mother's prayers. It was a wall of prayer warriors holding the line.

They won.

People began to ask, "Who is this woman who can stop a voodoo ceremony with just prayer?" My mom always gave the same answer: "I didn't stop anything. Who am I to stop such a thing? It was the Holy Spirit in me."

She never claimed credit. Never sought praise. She simply said: "No one who serves God will ever be put to shame. You might walk through shameful moments, but in the end, God lifts you up."

For my mother, grace wasn't just a word. It was a holy and undeserved gift she got to call hers. She had grown up with nothing, unable to read for the first five decades of her life, crushed by poverty, yet grace was enough.

That night I stopped seeing prayer as something you turn to only in times of crisis, like car insurance. Instead, I began to see it as a fuel line—an active, vital connection between ordinary people like my mom and the Master of the Universe.

CHAPTER 9

Escaped

Most of us have a favorite word, a word we repeat so often it might become unconsciously annoying to others. For my mom, that word was *grace*. You could hardly hear her pray without her mentioning it. To her, grace wasn't just an add-on; it was foundational. A gift none of us could ever afford, yet she taught us to cherish it as life's greatest blessing.

While my mom couldn't give us many material things, she pointed all of us to Jesus in ways I've rarely seen in other families in Pianotte or even in all of Haiti.

I know that may sound pretentious, but if you meet my mom, you'll quickly understand why I make such a bold claim. She's not just a source of inspiration; she's the foundation of my faith, my perseverance, and my understanding of what it means to trust God wholeheartedly.

In many Christian households, people go to church once a week, offer their prayers, and then continue with their lives. But for my mother, faith was as essential as breathing. She prayed every day, whispering her conversations with God as if He were sitting right next to her, often falling asleep mid-prayer.

To my mother, faith wasn't about denominations, doctrines, or church traditions. It was about trusting in Jesus, and that was what she instilled in me above all else. She taught all of her children the meaning of God's grace and encouraged us to live a life centered around that grace and His faithfulness. My siblings and I served in different church capacities throughout our childhood. In Gris-Gris, two of my sisters sang in the choir, and my older brother played the guitar.

Our house was never quiet. When the radio wasn't on, you could usually hear my mom singing a hymn. Sometimes the hymn was a popular one known by others. Other times, it was one she simply made up. All with one goal: to glorify Jesus in her waking hours.

Our home was small and modest, just a one-bedroom structure that, at night, became a two-bedroom: one room for the adults, the other for the children. My siblings and I often fell asleep to the soft murmur of my mother's voice, speaking to God with the kind of familiarity that only comes from a lifelong relationship. Because she was known throughout our town as a prayer warrior, my mother trusted in God's power to heal, provide, and protect. Her faith wasn't blind; it was anchored in conviction.

But the paradox of my mother's life, and what challenged me most as a young believer, was why someone so faithful endured so much hardship. If God truly rewards faith, why did we live with so many struggles? Why did we often go to bed hungry? Why did we lack basic necessities?

And most troubling of all, why did my mother suffer from an unexplained illness that no doctor could diagnose? For decades, my mother endured sudden, severe seizures that only happened at night. During the day, she was completely fine, full of energy, active, and engaged with life. But once or twice a month, without warning, she would lose consciousness in the middle of the night. Her body would go rigid, and she'd grind her teeth uncontrollably, her face locked in a pained expression. No matter how loudly we called her name, she wouldn't wake up.

She never complained and trusted that God would heal her, even though the seizures persisted for years. My mom saw her life as a layover, not the final destination. No traveler expects to linger in an airport forever; they know they're on their way to a better place. My mom understood that. She refused to feel miserable during her layover here on earth. Instead, she kept her eyes fixed on the destination: eternity.

She would not let her heart be troubled when things got difficult. She trusted that she had a reservation in heaven. Among her favorite Bible verses, the first four verses of John 14 were ones she treasured:

"Do not let your hearts be troubled. You believe in God; believe also in me. My Father's house has many rooms; if that were not so, would I have told you that I am going there to prepare a place for you? And if I go and prepare a place for you, I will come back and take you to be with me that you also may be where I am. You know the way to the place where I am going." **John 14:1–4 (NIV).**

Since she spoke to God regularly, we knew she had already brought this illness before Him. She trusted in His miraculous power, yet we also turned to medical care. In our family, those two sources of healing were never mutually exclusive. We took her to every hospital we could afford, consulting doctors, nurses, and specialists. But every test came back normal. No one could explain what was happening. Over time, my family stopped searching for medical explanations and began to suspect that something else was at play.

If this was truly an illness, why did it only happen at night? Why did it never occur when she was around other people? And why did it seem to grow worse as her faith deepened? Then, one day, one of my uncles approached my mother with a proposition that shook us.

In Haiti, it's commonly believed that some illnesses aren't medical but spiritual. Some say they're caused by ancestral spirits, known as Loa, demanding loyalty, or by curses placed by others. My uncle was convinced that my mother's seizures weren't physical, but spiritual. He told her that an ancestral spirit was calling her to serve, and that unless she embraced voodoo, the seizures would continue for the rest of her life.

He urged her to leave Christianity behind and devote herself to the ancestral spirits. My mother's response? Just two words:

"No way."

Her rejection was immediate, absolute, and irreversible. Despite all the suffering, despite the terrifying episodes, despite the fear that she might not survive the next seizure, she never wavered in her faith. Her voice carried John 14:1–4 through every corner of our small house. Those words were her anthem, held tight like a running back clutching the ball, daring anyone to take it away. She never wanted to trade her faith for half-baked, short-lived relief, no matter how much she suffered.

Then one night in 1999, everything changed.

That night, my mother had another seizure, but this time, it didn't follow the usual pattern. She didn't regain consciousness by dawn. The seizure hadn't taken its normal night path. Morning came, and we were still calling her name with no response. Normally, the episodes would pass before our day began at five a.m. But this time was different. This one had taken another route. We realized this would be a different day.

By morning, panic had set in. At six a.m., we all got up and started brainstorming what to do next. My sister lit the fire and brewed the morning coffee. In our household, coffee was usually the morning meal. We didn't drink it for energy but to quiet the hunger until the next bite—if food showed up at all. Most days, the coffee pot emptied before it had a chance to cool. But not that day. No one reached for a cup. No one needed warmth. What we needed were answers. Our minds were busy. In other words, our hearts were troubled.

Six-thirty a.m.

Seven a.m.

Seven-thirty a.m.

She was still unresponsive. By eight, we were desperate and terrified. Someone suggested calling the *Church Ladies,* my mother's closest friends. Prayer warriors who had spent decades interceding for others. One by one, they arrived at our house.

By ten-forty-five a.m., the small bedroom was packed with more than twenty women, all praying, loudly, passionately, relentlessly. They prayed with such force it felt like a battle, not against illness, but against something unseen.

They asked any family members who wanted to join them to commit fully. Come in and shut the door. No distractions.

When the *Church Ladies* prayed, there were no breaks for water, no pauses for lunch. They weren't praying for something; it was more like a group of friends trying to shake some sense into another: *'What the heck are you doing, Lord? We need answers!'*

Lunch time came and went, and all I could hear were the loud prayers coming from behind the closed door. These were the days when we had to listen to the radio for the time; we didn't have a clock in the house.

Two p.m. Still praying.

Three p.m.? No updates.

To us, that non-stop praying was a sign that the conversation with God was only getting more intense. Then, without warning, the noise fell silent. The door stayed shut. We leaned in, ears pressed tight against the wood, listening for whatever had caused the stillness. Then one of my sisters whispered, she was sure she could hear our mother's voice. We all froze. That had to be a good sign.

Sometime between three and four p.m., after hours of relentless intercession, my mother suddenly woke up.

Her first words?

"What's going on?" she asked. "Why are you all here?" After we explained what had happened, she simply said:

"It was quite a ride." And then she told us everything she had seen. In her vision, my mother saw herself trapped inside an iron cage, surrounded by a group of strange old men who mocked her. They told her they had been after her for decades but had never been able to capture her, until now. She realized they were celebrating her defeat. But then, something shifted. As they laughed, she began to recite Psalm 23:

"The Lord is my shepherd, I lack nothing... Even though I walk through the darkest valley, I will fear no evil, for you are with me..."

The men mocked her even more. So, she began to sing, a song she had never heard before, a song that simply came to her.

"My God, my God, do not let my enemies shame me."

As she sang, she felt herself changing. Her body transformed into a small bird, and just like that, she slipped through the cage's bars and flew away.

She escaped.

When she woke up she was breathless, but free. The room erupted in praise, with shouts of Hallelujah filling the space. That was the last seizure she ever had. What changed? Doctors had no explanation. But my mother had no doubt, it was God's intervention. To this day, she knows, deep in her soul, that it was God's grace that freed her.

There is no limit to God's grace.

That moment shaped not only my mother's life, but mine as well. It taught me that faith isn't about convenience; it's about conviction. It showed me that God doesn't always remove hardships immediately, but He always has a plan. It proved to me that the power of prayer is real. My mother's faith is the cornerstone of my life. Grace didn't just heal her; it raised all of us. Because of her, I will never stop believing.

That day, I realized the meal of faith my mother served us at home had nourished me far more than any church ever could. Grace didn't just set my mother free. It made us witnesses to a miracle. That day, I stopped just believing in God; I began to believe He hears.

CHAPTER 10
Broken Glass

In my family, the older children were always given priority when it came to going to school. The reasoning was simple: If the older ones could finish their education and secure a job, they could help support the rest of the family. It was a strategic sacrifice that shaped how we all viewed opportunity.

As a teenager I was naturally good at math, though I wouldn't make that claim today. Back then my skills caught the attention of Joe's family, a businessman from Port-au-Prince who visited my small town every few years.

Someone had mentioned me to him, and one afternoon he pulled up to my house in a gray Mitsubishi Pajero with his driver. He stepped out wearing cargo shorts so crisp they looked fresh off the rack, and on his feet, real leather Birkenstocks that gleamed softly in the sun. He looked rich. For a place like Pianotte, he was indeed wealthy.

He struck up a conversation with me, sizing me up in his own way. "I heard you're good at math. Maybe there's a future ahead for you," he said. Later that night, my mother pulled me aside and asked a life-changing question:

"Would you like to move to Port-au-Prince to live with Joe?"

I said yes.

At just eleven, I packed my things and left home, barely having a moment to process such a big decision. I didn't have time to think it through. Truthfully, at that age I didn't have the capacity for deep and complex processing anyway. Still, I had agreed to something that meant being separated from my family for the first time. I had never lived away from my parents and siblings. Part of my heart ached with uncertainty and sadness, while another part bounced with excitement at the thought of visiting Port-au-Prince, the famous city I'd heard so much about.

From 1995 to 1999, between the ages of eleven and fifteen, I lived in Port-au-Prince under Joe's roof. In just over two weeks, I went from chasing soccer balls made out of socks and banana leaves to walking on pavement and reaching into a

Frigidaire for ice. I had never touched anything that cold in my life. It felt as foreign as the city itself.

Many children in Haiti were sent to live away from home under a system known as *restavèk,* a term derived from the French *Reste Avec,* meaning "stay with." *Restavèk* was just a lighter euphemism for something much heavier: child slavery. The system had been around for generations. Poor families, hoping for a better future, sent their children to live with others, often strangers or distant relatives who were better off financially. These children did the kind of work most wouldn't ask their own sons or daughters to do. Things like scrubbing floors, hauling water, washing clothes, and cooking meals. While the children of the house laughed and played, the *restavèk* worked in the background. Many were beaten. Most ate only when allowed, and even then, they were given food made separately, never from the family's pot.

I often wonder if I was a *restavèk.* Technically, my situation checked nearly every box. I was sent away to live with someone who wasn't a relative. I did chores. However, I wasn't abused, and I never went hungry while living under his roof. Maybe if child slavery were a category, I'd qualify by circumstance, not by suffering. That's the tension I carry with me even as I am typing these words.

Before I moved in with Joe, I barely knew him. He was a strict man, always wearing a belt that served more than one purpose. He gave directions once, clear and measured, like a carpenter drawing a chalk line. But when my steps drifted off course, his leather belt came swinging like a hammer, jolting me back into alignment.

Still, Joe wasn't a bad person.

After all, corporal punishment wasn't a new concept to me. He fed me well, sheltered me, and handed me responsibilities that showed he trusted me. He owned a boutique, a small convenience store near the heart of downtown Port-au-Prince that sold cigarettes, cooking oil, butter, bread, and other basic necessities.

My job was to run the store every day from six in the morning until ten or eleven at night, depending on how busy things were. I was also responsible for collecting drinking water for the store and the house, pushing a wheelbarrow loaded with ten gallons of water for twenty minutes each trip, doing this once or twice a day. It was a nice house, located at Number 44 near Portail Leogane, one of the most populated sections of town. The years when I was living with Joe were some of the most confusing and challenging of my life.

I had to adjust to city life quickly and with little preparation. Life in Port-au-Prince was fast-paced, and even the accents people spoke with were slightly different from what I was used to in Pianotte. Some of the words we used in my village didn't make much sense here.

Port-au-Prince was confusing in many ways. While voodoo was familiar, many people also feared other things, like armed robbery, and people being shot or killed.

Back in Pianotte, we never heard of anyone dying from gunfire. If someone died, there were usually only two possible explanations: natural causes or voodoo. Port-au-Prince added another layer of complexity to an already complicated life.

Before I could be trusted to run the store on my own, Joe gave me a few ground rules. First, certain items were not to be sold after dark, like soap and sewing needles. Second, if I encountered anything that resembled a voodoo expedition, I was to stop and call Joe to handle it. These rules were his way of protecting the store from voodoo spells. He explained that, from time to time, he'd find strange objects left at the gate, signs of voodoo rituals. People with money were sometimes targeted by voodoo spells, often out of jealousy. At Joe's boutique, it wasn't unusual to find a voodoo artifact left by the door early in the morning or late at night after closing. So, I carefully listened to Joe's ground rules. I wasn't scared. I had some preliminary, though limited, knowledge of the voodoo world.

One day I was pushing the wheelbarrow, carrying water like I had done thousands of times before. As I passed through the neighborhood, I heard a loud boom. Turning my head I saw a black Mercedes with a shattered windshield parked next to a shop that sold ice. The entire street gasped.

I'd walked past that house more times than I could count, and that car was always there, settled like part of the landscape.

I didn't know Mercedes was a luxury brand, and even if I had, I wouldn't have reacted the way the bystanders did. To them, the broken windshield was a tragedy. To me, it was just glass. I didn't pause. I didn't log the moment away in my mind. It wasn't my car. It wasn't my story. I picked up my wheelbarrow and kept moving.

The cause, as everyone saw it, was a young boy with special needs who had thrown a rock. That evening, a husband-and-wife couple showed up at Joe's house.

"Your boy was teasing my son," they said.

I recognized the father, but the mother was unfamiliar. I was confused and scared. I could hear them talking to Joe outside while I was inside the boutique, helping customers and counting out change. But my mind was straining to catch pieces of whatever was unfolding out there. I tried to focus, making sure I didn't hand back too much or too little. But then I heard my name again, twice.

Voices rising.

And just like that, my heart started pounding, like it had been hooked up to a power line, surging with more voltage than it could handle.

And suddenly, they left.

Before I could say a word, Joe ordered me to go kneel in his bedroom and wait for my punishment. Kneeling always came before a beating. He didn't ask questions. He assumed I was guilty. When he walked in, he said nothing. He grabbed his belt and whipped me, for what felt like forever, though it lasted only about three minutes. Even after the belt stopped, the sting lingered longer than usual.

The next morning, the husband returned, this time demanding that Joe pay for the damage. They issued a threat: If he refused, they would go to a witch doctor and cast a spell on me.

Joe refused.

"Junior didn't do it. I'm not paying you a dime."

"We'll recoup our money one way or another," the man muttered as he left. Joe called me into his room that night and spoke in a grave tone. "Those people are from Anse-a-Veau," he warned, "a town in Haiti known for strong voodoo rituals. If you did tease that boy, I'd be mad, but I'd pay the money. But if they go to the witch doctor… you'll be dead." A tight knot twisted in my stomach, freezing every word I wanted to say. It was like my mind had been wiped clean, a sudden blank slate where nothing could take shape.

I was terrified, but I managed to get the words out, and for the first time, my voice was firm and loud. "I swear to God, I didn't do it. I swear. I swear."

I had heard stories of people being killed by voodoo expeditions, but this was the first time I was at the center of one. There are unspoken rules in voodoo that every Haitian knew, even a young boy like me. I grew up with the saying, *"Asire ou ke konsyans ou klè"*, translated as: Be sure you have a clean conscience. In other words, those who are blameless cannot be harmed by a voodoo expedition. In my case, if I wasn't the one who threw the rock, then I was blameless. But if I was lying, a voodoo expedition meant to harm me would easily find its way in. It was the Haitian equivalent of "The truth will set you free." Knowing I didn't throw the rock gave me a clean conscience. Still, that alone wasn't enough to calm the fear in the mind of a thirteen-year-old being threatened with voodoo and death.

The man came back one more time. This time, it felt final. When he entered the boutique, he didn't speak to me; he simply called out Joe's name. His speech was long and winding, but the message was clear: Pay for the damage now, or deal with the consequences.

Joe refused again.

"Hey, listen, my boy is innocent. Do what you must, but we owe you nothing. Give me a break."

Hearing those words terrified me to my core. I knew I was innocent, but fear took over. I was afraid someone might kill me, either through a spell or by ambushing me the next time I went to fetch water. I couldn't sleep. For days, fear consumed me. And there was no way to tell my mother, who was nearly a hundred miles away.

CHAPTER 11
Inches Away

On the ninth day after being threatened with a voodoo curse, I was walking downtown and crossed a street I knew like the back of my hand. Two black plastic bags hung from my fingers, heavy with fresh vegetables for Joe. The street felt unusually still, like the city was holding its breath. I looked right, no cars. Left, still no cars. I stepped forward into the space. Out of nowhere, a large white Coca-Cola truck came speeding toward me.

I froze.

The truck missed me by inches. The space between the front bumper and my ribcage was so tight, it couldn't have held a deck of cards. Before I could even process what had happened, I was surrounded by people. The screeching tires and the sound of hundreds of glass bottles crashing had drawn a crowd.

The driver jumped out, pale and shaken. His eyes locked onto mine, wide with disbelief that pressed down like a heavy weight. His hands landed on my shoulders, steady, but hesitant. He shook his head in every direction, speechless. His silence said more than words ever could.

"Who the hell are you, kid? I swear to God, I didn't see you!" said the driver, speaking loudly with a cracked voice. As he walked away to assess the damage of hundreds of broken bottles, he took one good look at me and said with a stern look on his face:

"Kid, if you're a Christian, keep serving God. If you serve the spirits, keep serving them. Because whatever saved you today, it was grace."

In that moment, I realized something profound: They sent a voodoo spell in my direction, yet it didn't take hold because I was blameless. The truth has set me free.

That same night, the special-needs boy who had thrown the rock died suddenly. Many believed it was because I told the truth, and the spell reversed. I didn't know what to believe, but I knew this: Something supernatural had happened. I was alive for one reason: God's grace.

After the voodoo incident, something shifted between Joe and me. Joe was a believer, but like many Haitians, he also dabbled in voodoo. He started to trust me more. Even though I was still a teenager, he began treating me differently. I was bright, honest, and still great at math, which made me useful to him.

I was no longer just a kid working in the store; I was his right-hand man. Every morning, I opened the boutique at six a.m., left for school, then returned to work through the night. Even with the added trust, the shadow of the belt never disappeared. Trust didn't subtract from his strict discipline, not one bit.

I had been in the city for roughly two years by then, and life had its ups and downs. The bright side? I wasn't going hungry. Joe made sure of that. He fed me like I was his own, not just someone staying in the house. Those were some of the healthiest years of my life, physically speaking. I always had a plate of food and a roof over my head. That part was good.

But it was my first time being away from home, and some nights I missed my family so much it felt like something heavy had dropped on my chest. I'd have dreams about Gris-Gris, being with my siblings, hearing my mom's voice, just doing life like we used to. Then I'd wake up and remember I was one hundred miles away from reality. In a country with such precarious infrastructures, I may well be on another planet.

There was no calling home. No internet. Just silence. I had to wait for someone, really anyone, coming from Gris-Gris to the city. And that didn't happen often. Usually once a year,

Joe's cousin would make the trip. That was my moment. I'd light up like it was a holiday.

He lived near my mother's house in Pianotte, so I treated him like my human voicemail. I'd ask about everyone, starting with Mom and Dad, then my siblings, one by one. He always answered patiently, filling in every detail I could think to ask. Those visits were like fuel. They carried me for months and even years. But no matter how many updates I got, it never satisfied the deeper longing just to see their faces again.

After every fresh Gris-Gris download with Joe's cousin, I'd sneak away to the wooden shed behind the house, curling up next to that half-finished cement-block wall and cried like crazy. There, my tears would pour like a faucet stuck wide open, and no matter how much I tried, they just wouldn't stop. It wasn't easy to say out loud why I felt so broken, but later I understood. Even though for the first time in my life I had my own bed at Joe's house, a big part of me would rather sleep on the cement floor in Pianotte with my siblings, who had this crazy way of kicking me awake, sometimes on purpose, sometimes just in their sleep. I never breathed a word to Joe about how much I missed home. I kept it all in. I didn't want to risk him sending me back to Gris-Gris because I know I would have some explaining to do to my parents. Also, I didn't want him to start doubting whether he could trust me. So, with everything at stake, I played cool.

As Joe's confidence in me grew, he brought in another boy from my hometown. His name was Jude. He was my cousin from Pianotte. His job was to help with cleaning, landscaping, and collecting water. I ran the store. Joe sent us both to school, but Jude and I didn't attend the same one. I went to Lycée Toussaint Louverture, a well-known public school in Port-au-Prince. Jude went to evening classes at a school a few miles away.

Unlike me, Jude was carefree. He loved to play and have fun. I was focused on school and getting good grades. We lived in the same house, but we were on different paths. One of us was chasing a future beyond Port-au-Prince; the other was still figuring out what that future might look like. Jude wasn't a bad person; he was family. He just loved partying and buying name-brand secondhand clothes like Fila, Reebok, and FUBU.

For months, Jude snuck out at night and came back with stories of fun. He kept trying to get me to join him, but I always said no. It didn't sound like fun to me; it sounded like trouble waiting to happen.

But in February of 1999, after relentless persuasion, I gave in. He wanted to sneak out to the annual carnival festival that took place in Port-au-Prince. Carnival, or Mardi Gras, as we called it, was three days of all-night celebrations, with thousands crowding the streets of the capital to enjoy and dance to some of Haiti's most popular musical bands.

Back then, Mardi Gras in Haiti was dangerous. Tens of thousands gathered, and some came only to cause chaos. People carried razor blades and knives, slicing through crowds and leaving injuries behind. If you weren't careful you could end up in the hospital, or worse.

Still, I agreed.

It was Sunday night, the first night of Mardi Gras. The air was thick and restless. Joe went to bed at ten. Twenty minutes later, Jude and I tried to sneak out. We avoided the red metal gate, it made too much noise. Climbing felt safer.

I was almost over when the light came on. I froze. Then I heard him.

Joe, in his pajamas, was already on his way out, and we had nowhere to hide.

"Who's there? Junior, is that you? What are you doing? Are you serious?"

My heart stopped. The first time I tried to sneak out, I got caught. I was mortified.

"You gotta be kidding me. This is it. Junior, I trusted you," Joe said, shaking his head.

He launched into a long speech about how dangerous Carnival was, how people got killed there. Within 48 hours, he sent us both home.

Back in Pianotte, my parents were disappointed, especially my mother. She had raised us in poverty, but she made sure we were rich in character.

She looked at me with quiet disappointment and said,

"Make sure poor is the only negative word people use to describe you. I don't want to hear liar, cheater, thief. Poor, that's the only one I'll accept."

They put me back in school, but life wasn't the same. With Joe, hunger wasn't a thing. But in Pianotte, the harsh reality of a destitute life returned.

In Haiti, students prayed that schools would provide uniforms. They were the great equalizer. When everyone wore the same thing, no one could tell who was rich or poor. But without a uniform, people noticed.

I went to school with just one black-and-white composition notebook, the only thing I could afford. Finding shoes, food, or even basic supplies was a struggle.

I looked around and saw my peers with backpacks, while I had to sit beside a friend just to share books and avoid looking ashamed or out of place.

Being back in Pianotte stirred up a cocktail of feelings in me. I was sad leaving behind a city where streetlights automatically turned on most nights. A city where cars honked nonstop and people I knew watched TV and ate three meals a day. At Joe's, I never had to wonder about my next meal. Three meals a day had become normal, like clockwork, and that alone felt like more than a simple *touchdown*. It was more like scoring a touchdown, nailing the field goal, and scoring the extra point all in one possession.

Still, under the weight of all that "loss," my heart was secretly doing cartwheels. I had missed my family so much it hurt. I tried to wear the face of a disappointed son, one who knew he was giving up comfort, but the grin on my face was hard to hide. When I compared what I'd walked away from with what was waiting for me back home, it was no contest. If it were a football game between comfort in the city against being with my family in Pianotte, my family would have won in a landslide.

Pianotte didn't waste time reminding me I wasn't in the city anymore. One day I was flipping light switches; the next, I was lighting kerosene lamps. At home, there was no luxury, no buzz of power lines, no hum of appliances. Still, I returned with something far richer: a deeper faith and a clearer vision of who I was becoming.

CHAPTER 12

An Unexpected Offer

There are moments heaven weaves into our lives so gently, we almost miss them: a conversation, a quiet nudge, a door barely cracked open.

This is the story of how a dream, a God-orchestrated meeting, and a man named Mike became the beginning of a future I couldn't have imagined.

After living with Joe, I found myself back in Pianotte, trying to make sense of what might come next. That's when I first met the missionaries from Minnesota. They came once or twice a year, bringing help and building relationships with the people of Gris-Gris. At first, they were just kind visitors, people who came and went. But over time, their presence became something more: a bridge to a future I never saw coming.

Even before I lived with Joe, I was fascinated by language. My love for language started with our old crank radio. Every day, Voice of America would come through in Creole, and certain names came around again and again. Names like Bill Clinton, Margaret Thatcher, and Nelson Mandela came up so often, they felt like distant relatives. I didn't realize it then, but listening to those translated voices, people speaking a language I didn't know, was my first glimpse into a much bigger world. That's when something in me shifted, and I started falling in love with language.

Every time the missionaries came to town, they brought interpreters, people who could bridge the gap between two worlds, translating not just words but entire cultures. I watched in awe as the interpreters moved seamlessly between Creole and English, making sure both sides truly understood each other. To me, it was a skill filled with power. The power to connect, to explain, to help people see from different perspectives.

I wanted to be one of them. I wanted to be the person standing between two people who couldn't otherwise communicate, helping their words find meaning across languages. After all, interpreters do more than translate words. They bridge worlds. I fell in love with the idea of becoming one. But learning English cost money, and money was something I didn't have. Still I held onto my dream, though deep down it felt impossible.

Until the day Mike approached me. Without knowing much about me, he said, "I feel like God is telling me I need to help you." I was stunned. He didn't know me. I didn't know him. How could he possibly help me? Then he said something that didn't just land in my ears; it landed in my spirit: "You see, in Haiti, if you become an interpreter, you can make good money."

I couldn't believe what I was hearing. This was my dream. But how did he know? How was it possible that a complete stranger, who had no reason to approach me, was speaking directly to the secret hope I had carried for years? But Mike wasn't finished. "Let's make a deal," he said. "You look like a bright young man. I think you have a bright future ahead of you if you study hard and keep God in your heart. What if I could pay for you to go to school?"

All of this was being translated through an interpreter. The few seconds between Mike's words and the translation into Creole were filled with pounding heartbeats and unbelievable anticipation. At first, I thought he was joking. Why would someone who didn't even know me suddenly offer to change my life?

So I asked: "How would you do that?"

"It would be like a student loan. You know what that is?" I had no idea what those two words meant. Mike didn't hesitate. "Well, how much do you think it would cost?" I had no clue. I'd never even dared to ask how much English classes might cost. So, I blurted out the biggest number I could imagine:

"One hundred dollars."

To me, that was an enormous amount of money. When Mike asked the interpreter to translate my answer, the interpreter chuckled before speaking. Then he turned to me and said,

"That's not even close."

He explained that learning English properly, with tuition, books, transportation, and materials, would cost thousands of dollars. I was stunned. I had never even considered a number that high. It felt so far out of reach that, for a moment, my dream seemed impossible all over again.

But Mike wasn't discouraged. Instead, he smiled and said,

"Go find out. Do the research. Figure out how much it would take for you to truly learn English. Then come back and tell me." As I walked away, my chest tightened with a wild mix of eagerness and doubt, like standing on the edge of a cliff I wasn't sure I was ready to jump from. Could this really happen? Could I actually learn English? Could this man, who had no reason to help me, truly be offering to change my future? I didn't know the answers. But for the first time, I had a reason to try.

An Unexpected Offer

I was just shy of eighteen when I met Mike. Once I got home, I started looking into English schools in Port-au-Prince. My "research" was nothing more than asking around. Most people I asked would laugh; some waved me off. They knew I couldn't pay for a school like that. Asking around and trying to find a credible English school felt like staring at the sky, wondering if I could ever set foot on Mars. At the time, I was as broke as could be. I had nothing to my name. My only "assets" amounted to half a goat, thanks to a practice known around Pianotte as a 50/50 deal. Someone with money bought the goat, and I cared for it. After a year, we'd split the value. If the goat happened to produce kids, one would be mine outright. It was a slow path to ownership, but it was something. The following picture was taken on the very day I met Mike.

Mike's offer wasn't just about money. It was about belief—belief in me. A belief I hadn't even discovered in myself yet. That moment set everything in motion. It was the first step in a journey that would eventually take me from Port-au-Prince to the United States, specifically Minnesota, and from the dream of becoming an interpreter to a reality I never thought possible.

Looking back now, I realize that Mike's decision to help me wasn't just a kind gesture. It was a divine appointment. It was God's way of showing me that even when a dream feels out of reach, He can place the right people in your path to make it possible. That single conversation changed everything, and it was only the beginning.

I was overjoyed, pumped, and full of excitement. For the first time in my life, I could see my dream turning into reality. With Mike's incredible generosity, the door had finally opened. But I had one big problem: I was still living in Gris-Gris. In Haiti, the best schools, especially those offering a strong English education, were located in Port-au-Prince. If I wanted to make this happen, I had no choice but to move back to the capital.

The idea of moving to Port-au-Prince a second time was both exciting and terrifying. The first time I went to the city, I was barely a teenager. Back then, Port-au-Prince was relatively stable. The country was experimenting with democracy, and President Jean-Bertrand Aristide was serving his first term.

At the time, the economy was improving, the streets were clean, people felt safer, and there was a sense of political stability. But this time, things were very different. As I prepared for my second move in 2003, Haiti was descending into turmoil.

President Aristide had been re-elected for a second term, but his presidency was marked by political unrest and economic hardship. The cost of food skyrocketed, pushing more people into poverty. Armed groups took to the streets, demanding Aristide's resignation. Violence, riots, and instability became the norm.

Moving to Port-au-Prince at that time was dangerous, but I had no choice. This was my one chance to chase my dream, and I wasn't going to let fear hold me back.

I reached out to a close friend, someone I trusted deeply, but will keep anonymous for the sake of this story. I explained that I had been given a golden opportunity to study in Port-au-Prince, but I needed help finding a place to live.

His response was simple and generous:

"You can live with me."

I was relieved. Knowing I had a safe place to stay gave me the courage to push forward, despite the chaos unfolding in the city.

My friend lived in Carrefour, a densely populated area on the southern edge of Port-au-Prince, just outside downtown. It was a central hub where people from all over Haiti lived. Even though it was crowded, it was considered safer than other parts of the city. Best of all, it was relatively close to where I wanted to study.

Meanwhile, I was researching the real cost of learning English. The numbers were nowhere near my original estimate. For two years of study, including tuition, books, and transportation, I would need at least $2,150. That was more than twenty times what I had guessed.

An Unexpected Offer

I had been given an incredible opportunity, but it came with challenges I hadn't prepared for. Still, I had come too far to turn back now.

CHAPTER 13

Bouncing on Charcoal

The road from Gris-Gris to Port-au-Prince was just as long, rough, and uncomfortable as it had been the first time. In Haiti, most people travel by tap-taps, colorfully decorated trucks or buses that serve as public transport. They're often overcrowded, packed with passengers, bags of charcoal, livestock, and goods for the market. But I didn't ride in a tap-tap.

My journey to Port-au-Prince took fourteen hours with delays, in a truck that carried only charcoal. Thankfully, I didn't have to pay for the trip. One of my cousins worked for a transportation company and managed to find me a spot to ride for free. These large trucks were used to exclusively haul goods from the countryside to the capital. That day, the big truck rocked from side to side, crawling no faster than someone on foot. I had no company except a few dozen noisy chickens and a great view from my seat on top of the hard and dirty charcoal. The truck groaned under the weight of charcoal, packed to the brim with no room to breathe.

For the entire ride, I was bouncing uncomfortably, inhaling dust, and trying to ignore the heat and exhaustion. I was chasing something more valuable than comfort: a future worth pursuing. I was determined, because every mile I traveled brought me closer to the future I had always dreamed of. I left my hometown under a moonlit sky, sometime between midnight and one in the morning.

When I finally arrived in Port-au-Prince, I stepped into a city I barely recognized. Gone were the clean streets and the relative safety I had experienced a few years earlier. Instead, I was met with burning tires from political protests, a heavy police presence, and armed civilians. The city had transformed, charged with tension, anger, danger, and desperation. Now, in addition to getting an education, I had to survive in a place that felt like it was on the brink of collapse. I didn't know if I'd make it through this next chapter of my life. But one thing I knew for sure: I wasn't giving up. I was stepping into uncertainty, facing challenges I wasn't prepared for, and trusting that God had a plan for me even if I couldn't see it yet.

I arrived in Port-au-Prince, exhausted from the fourteen-hour journey, ready to start my new life. Everything had been carefully planned. Or so I thought.

I was supposed to meet my friend at a Texaco gas station in Carrefour, where he would take me to my new home. But when I arrived, he wasn't there. At first, I thought he was just running late. I waited. Hours passed. I waited some more. The sun began its slow descent, and with every passing minute, my excitement turned into worry. Still, he never showed up. Desperate, I borrowed a phone from a stranger, the only way I could reach him. When he picked up, his voice carried both anxiety and regret.

"Hey man, how do I say this… I'm so sorry," he said. "I can't host you anymore."

Everything changed in an instant. He'd been kicked out and was now staying with a friend who barely had space for himself, let alone me. For a moment, everything went blurry, and my mind started racing. I had a little bit of money in my pocket, but every cent was budgeted for transportation to school. Now I was in the city with nowhere to go. And just like that, the plan I had been counting on crumbled.

A storm rose inside me— uncertainty, fear, and disappointment all bubbling to the surface. I was shaken, but not frozen. I stood alone in a city in turmoil, beneath a gas station canopy, with nowhere to go, no one expecting me, and no backup plan. I was stranded in a city that had become dangerous. Carrefour was overcrowded and chaotic, filled with thousands of people struggling to survive. Violence was everywhere: muggings, kidnappings, and political unrest.

The sun was setting, and it wasn't safe to be out after dark. In a city on edge, the sun's exit didn't just darken the streets, it changed them. It unlocked a different kind of life, where danger crept out of hiding and the night belonged to those who dealt in fear.

I had everything I owned with me: a bag of charcoal, plantains, cooking oil, flour, and other goods I had brought from Gris-Gris to help set up my new home. But now, there was no home. I couldn't just leave my belongings behind to search for shelter. In a city like Carrefour, if you leave something unattended, it's as good as gone. So there I was, standing in the middle of chaos, carrying everything I owned with no idea what to do next.

As darkness crept closer, panic rose in my chest. Sleeping under the gas station was out of the question. I could be robbed. I could be beaten. I could be kidnapped. There was a real possibility I could be killed. I had to find someone, anyone, who might be able to help me.

I didn't own a cell phone, and I hadn't spoken to most of my contacts in years. I sat down, grabbed a pen and a scrap of paper, and started making a list of everyone I knew in Port-au-Prince, searching my memory for names that might save me. The list was short. Just a few names.

I sifted through old memories, trying to recall anyone who might be willing or able, to help. My godmother lived in Carrefour, the same place where I was now stranded. But I hadn't seen or spoken to her in many years. I didn't know if I still had a place in her memory, let alone under her roof. Then there was my cousin. She lived in Tabarre, on the other side of the city. I had heard of her, but we hadn't spoken in years. I wasn't sure she would welcome me. Johnny, my former classmate from Gris-Gris, lived in Pétion-Ville, another part of the city. But I had no way to contact him. None of the names felt quite right, but I clung to them anyway.

Then, as I kept hitting the refresh button in my mind, one name stood out: Regine! She was my cousin, though we hadn't been close in a long time. Her mother and my father were siblings, which gave me something solid to hold on to. I knew she had a husband, two young boys, and a home in La Plaine, on the north side of Port-au-Prince.

I hadn't seen her in years. But when you're stranded, even the faintest thread of family can feel like a lifeline. Maybe, just maybe, she would remember me. Maybe she would let me stay. Maybe she was the answer to my prayers. As I gathered my belongings, preparing to find my way to Regine's house, my heart pounded with uncertainty. What if she wasn't home? What if she didn't recognize me? What if she refused to help? I didn't know what to expect. All I knew was that I had to try.

I took a deep breath, tightened my grip on my bags, and started walking. Whatever happened next would determine everything. With my belongings secured and my heart still racing, I hopped onto a tap-tap and made my way to Regine's house. I didn't know what to expect. Night was closing in fast, and while my body rested on the wooden bench inside the tap-tap, my mind was running wild, imagining how Regine might react. Would she open the door with a smile? Or not open it at all?

When I arrived, she greeted me as if no time had passed. She welcomed me as one of her own, offering a place to stay for as long as I needed. I was relieved. For the first time since arriving in Port-au-Prince, I could breathe. I had finally found shelter, but with it came a new challenge.

The English school was much farther than I had anticipated. From Regine's house, the commute took up to an hour and 45 minutes each way. To make matters worse, I had to pay for two separate rides just to get there. Each morning, I squeezed into crowded tap-taps, winding through the city's congested streets, unpredictable traffic, and frequent roadblocks triggered by protests and political unrest. By the time I arrived at school, I was already exhausted. But I didn't have a choice, I was there to learn.

My first experience living in Port-au-Prince as a teenager had been relatively comfortable. This time, life was much harder. Regine did everything she could to help me, but the reality was that she had her own struggles. Money was tight, and her resources were limited.

Just weeks before I arrived, Regine had lost her husband. She and her late husband had been middle-class Haitians living a fairly decent life. Over the years, they had built their own home in La Plaine. They owned a couple of vehicles and ran a small hardware store, so people in the neighborhood who needed simple things like PVC pipes, a sink, or a toilet bowl didn't have to travel all the way to downtown Port-au-Prince. When I arrived at Regine's house, she and her two boys were still mourning the loss.

Regine didn't charge me rent or ask me to help with daily expenses like food. I couldn't ask her for anything more. I was grateful for a roof over my head, but it was clear that this chapter of my life would be one of patience and sacrifice.

In addition to my English studies, I also enrolled in secondary school in Port-au-Prince. Thanks to Regine's connection, I was accepted into Lycée Guy Malary, a public school built in the late 1990s by President Jean-Bertrand Aristide. It was one of the closest schools to where I lived, which made it the most practical option. But the location of Guy Malary also meant something else: it placed me less than four miles from Cité Soleil, one of the largest and most dangerous slums in the country.

Many of my classmates at Guy Malary were from Cité Soleil. Through them, I gained a window into one of the deepest and most misunderstood parts of Haiti. For most people, Cité Soleil existed only in news reports, a place associated with poverty, gang violence, and desperation. Spanning less than nine square miles, it was estimated to house between 350,000 and 400,000 people, making it one of the most densely populated slums in the Western Hemisphere. Though just a few miles from Port-au-Prince's international airport, it felt like an entirely different world.

Cité Soleil hadn't always been called that. In the early 1960s, during Haiti's dictatorship years, it was originally named Cité Simone, after Simone Duvalier, the wife of Dictator François Duvalier, widely known throughout Haiti under the nickname "Papa Doc." Back then, the area was home to workers from the nearby HASCO sugarcane factory. It was a growing community of laborers making an honest living, not yet the crime-ridden slum it would later become. But as Haiti's economy crumbled and industries collapsed, poverty took over.

By the time I returned to Port-au-Prince for my second stay, Cité Soleil had become notorious for gang violence and political unrest. Yet despite its dark reputation, it had a life of its own. Inside the slum, neighborhoods had names that sounded oddly familiar: Boston, New York, Brooklyn. One of my closest friends lived in "Boston," one of the most dangerous areas within the slum. Two of my classmates who had become dear friends lived in Soleil 17, another zone most people in Port-au-Prince tried to avoid at all costs.

I was navigating two very different worlds at once: the world of education and dreams, and the world of struggle and survival. Through it all I held on to one thing: the belief that my dream was worth the struggle.

I was willing to endure long commutes, financial hardship, and uncertainty because I knew that learning English could change my future. Even if it meant waking up before dawn, squeezing onto overcrowded tap-taps, or studying late into the night, I was determined to make it work.

As I spent more time in Port-au-Prince, I came to understand something important: People are not defined by where they come from. Many of my classmates from Cité Soleil were some of the most hardworking, intelligent, and ambitious people I had ever met. They dreamed of better lives, just like I did. They wanted education, opportunity, and a future beyond the slums. Yet for many of them, leaving Cité Soleil was nearly impossible. Some would never escape the cycle of poverty.

CHAPTER 14
Major Adjustment

There's a running joke in Haiti: If you die a Haitian and never visited Port-au-Prince, God might send you back because that's an important life lesson you missed. If that's true, then I'll have extra credit in heaven.

Port-au-Prince was a city where life changed every day. The gap between those who were struggling and those who were thriving felt like the distance between continents. I was surrounded by people from every walk of life. The calm of Gris-Gris felt a world away compared to the city's fast, chaotic energy. It was overwhelming, but I was beginning to see the city with fresh eyes and a deeper understanding.

Many of my new friends in Cité Soleil invited me to events, gatherings, and community programs. For a young man who had spent most of his life in the mountains, these experiences were eye-opening. But as I quickly learned, the city had its own challenges, especially when it came to survival.

Back in Gris-Gris, even when food was scarce, there was always something we could do to get a morsel. If we were hungry, we could pick a mango off a tree. When mangoes weren't in season, we'd find a coconut, breadfruit, or banana. In desperate times, we fought the soil two or three times a day, hoping to find a sweet potato. Hunger in the countryside was different from hunger in the city.

In Port-au-Prince, when you were hungry, there was nothing free to eat. No trees to climb, no farmland to harvest, no way to survive unless you had money. Even paying the daily tap-tap fare was a challenge. On some days, I walked over ninety minutes one way just to attend class. Life was hard, but I was determined to keep going. Once I got to school, hungry or not, I was in my element. Adapting to hunger was only part of the adjustment. School had its own unexpected lessons in store.

One of the greatest influences during this time was my English professor, Mr. Lionel, better known to the students as Mr. Cash. He was passionate about teaching and had an energy that made learning exciting. He genuinely wanted his students to become fluent in English— not just to pass a test, but to truly master the language.

Mr. Cash had a unique way of introducing us to American culture. He brought in household items, from mirrors to silverware. It wasn't uncommon to walk into his class and find shampoo, conditioner, or other random items he felt we needed to know about. His teaching style was unconventional for Haiti, and that was what made him a renowned teacher both in our school and throughout the city. He explained holidays like Halloween and Thanksgiving, concepts that were completely foreign to us.

There was a rhythm to his teaching. Each day brought a new word; we called it WOD, short for "Word of the Day." But those words did more than build vocabulary. They stretched our thinking, quietly shaping how we saw the world. One particular lesson has stayed with me to this day. It was a Tuesday morning when Mr. Cash walked into the classroom, went straight to the chalkboard, and wrote a single word: DESSERT. I remember thinking, that's easy! A girl sitting next to me, full of confidence, shot her hand up, eager to answer before the wave of other hands that would surely follow.

"I know! I know! I know what that is!" she shouted.

But for Mr. Cash, it wasn't enough to just know the word. You had to explain it. In English. She smiled proudly and said, "Dessert is a place with no trees." Mr. Cash shook his head. "No, that's desert," he said. "This is something completely different." He waited for a few more answers, but it turned out many of us had been thinking the same thing. Then he wrote a second word on the board: APPETIZER.

The room fell silent. We stared at the new word the way someone might stare at a strange star in the sky, familiar, yet completely out of reach. I can still remember the way Mr. Cash laughed in disbelief. "None of you know what an appetizer is?" he asked. We all shook our heads.

"Unbelievable," he sighed.

Then he gave us an explanation that changed the way I understood both English and American culture:

"An appetizer is the food you eat before you eat. A dessert is the food you eat after you eat."

Phanord, who was sitting in the front row, raised his hand with a puzzled and slightly amused look on his face. "Wait. Wait... Mr. Cash, this makes no sense at all, sir. Then what do you call the food you eat in between?" The entire class burst into laughter.

To help us understand, Mr. Cash returned the next day with printed restaurant menus and walked us through real-life examples of appetizers and desserts. That day, I realized my journey wasn't just about learning a language; it was about decoding an entirely new culture.

There was a quiet sense of embarrassment among us, but deep down, we knew we were on the right track. Concepts like appetizers and desserts felt foreign, like pieces of a world we hadn't yet tasted. Still, we understood that what we were being served was knowledge and one day, it would nourish something greater in us.

Outside of class, I immersed myself in the language by spending time with a group of Haitian professionals who worked as interpreters for humanitarian organizations. These were people who had traveled across Haiti, working with foreigners and perfecting their English through real-world experience. They understood the power of language as a tool for opportunity. Every conversation I had with them expanded my vocabulary. Every interaction helped me refine my pronunciation. Slowly but surely, English was becoming easier for me.

Learning English and the intricacies of American culture wasn't the only education I was getting. Port-au-Prince was also teaching me valuable life lessons. Living in Port-au-Prince and spending time with people from Cité Soleil gave me a completely new understanding of survival, struggle, and resilience. The city had changed me. It sharpened my hunger, not just for food, but for knowledge, for perspective, for possibility. And despite the noise, the heat, and the hardship, I was learning how to survive in a world far bigger than Gris-Gris.

CHAPTER 15

Staring Down the Barrel of a Gun

By early 2004, Haiti had reached a boiling point. Violent protests, kidnappings, and gang control gripped Port-au-Prince, especially in places like Cité Soleil, where loyalty to President Aristide ran deep. During his second term, Aristide had built a strong base of supporters, many of whom remained fiercely devoted to him. But the country was divided. While some demanded his resignation, others flooded the streets in his support.

The divide between those who admired President Aristide and those who despised him was a frequent topic of conversation. Aristide, a former priest from southern Haiti, began gaining popularity in the late 1980s with his sermons against dictatorships. In addition to his theological studies, he possessed what many would call a gift for language. Having been born and raised in a poor region of Haiti, he knew how to convey his message to all classes of Haitians. His speeches were widely broadcast, and he spoke in ways that even those who were illiterate could easily understand. Unlike many other politicians of his time, he rarely spoke French, even though he often reminded people that he spoke more than six languages. He spoke plain Creole, free of the fancy French words most people of his rank used. The emblem of his political party, a rooster symbolizing a fighter, was a subtle message that he cared about the common poor Haitian. His message resonated, and many Haitians loved him. All over the country, people knew him as *"Titid,"* a nickname spoken with ease, and one that most Haitians tied to perhaps the most popular politician of my generation.

While he was admired by many, he was equally disliked by a large swath of the population. During his second term, he was accused of misappropriating funds and not truly caring about the poor. The tension between the two sides often spilled into violence, and too often, lives were lost in the chaos.

The first few weeks of the New Year brought a level of unrest that felt heavy, even for a country all too familiar with political turmoil. I could feel it; something had to give. The pot was close to boiling over, and I knew when that happened, it would spill straight into the fire.

It did.

On February 29, President Aristide resigned and left the country, heading into exile in the Central African Republic. When news of his resignation broke, anti-Aristide Haitians celebrated, while his supporters were devastated, and many turned violent.

For reasons I still don't fully understand, Cité Soleil had an unusually high concentration of pro-Aristide militants. So, when he went into exile, the neighborhood erupted. Gunfire echoed day and night, a relentless rhythm that became part of the air we breathed.

The president's departure sent Haiti into freefall, plunging the country into complete turmoil. The situation had spiraled so far out of control that the international community could no longer look away.

In a swift response, the UN Security Council voted to deploy a peacekeeping mission to Haiti. Within months, thousands of troops from around the world, including Africa, Central America, and the Caribbean, arrived in Port-au-Prince to patrol the streets and attempt to restore stability.

Yet despite their presence, the violence didn't stop. A kidnapping epidemic broke out. Even before the president's departure, kidnappings were already a terrifying reality in Haiti, an easy way for criminals to squeeze what little money families had. But after Aristide's resignation, the numbers skyrocketed. By March and April of 2004, Haiti was seeing up to a hundred kidnappings per day, just in Port-au-Prince alone. The kidnapping epidemic became a common tactic for the gangs, who would abduct people from the streets and demand ransom for their release. When the ransom wasn't paid, the hostage was often killed.

One of my classmates from the English Institute became a victim of this nightmare. She went missing for days. Then, her body was found in a pile of trash, discarded like garbage after her parents had failed to pay the fifteen thousand U.S. dollars the aggressors demanded. Despite the growing UN presence, the pro-Aristide gangs remained bold, sending a clear message: Bring the president back, or the violence continues.

Port-au-Prince by itself wasn't all of Haiti, but in moments like these, it felt like it was.

Some Haitians argued that the president had resigned voluntarily. Others were convinced his removal was an orchestrated coup by foreign governments. Regardless of the truth, one thing was certain: Port-au-Prince was on fire, and no one was safe.

Yet amid the chaos, life had to go on. Regine's store still needed restocking. And that's how we found ourselves planning a trip downtown, right into the eye of the storm.

The store itself was in a relatively safe area, but getting supplies meant heading into downtown Port-au-Prince. I never liked going there. We didn't have a vehicle large enough for the load, but one of our neighbors did. He agreed to take us in his white two-door pickup.

Before setting out, we had to choose our route carefully. One option cut through Cité Soleil, the epicenter of kidnappings and street violence. It was the fastest way downtown, but it also meant passing through one of the most dangerous areas in the city, perhaps even the country.

We all agreed: "We are not driving through Cité Soleil." We clearly communicated our preferred route to the driver and asked him to repeat it back, almost like air traffic controllers confirming flight instructions. But as we approached the intersection, the point where we had to choose between the safer, longer road and the quicker, riskier one, our driver hesitated.

"I think we'll be okay," he said. "Things look quiet. Here we go!" Against our better judgment, we took the dangerous route. I was sitting in the back seat, distracted, looking at my cousin's Nokia cell phone, one of those old models with an antenna and a battery that seemed to last forever. Then, suddenly, the car screeched to a halt.

I looked up and locked eyes with armed men, guns pointed directly at us.

I panicked.

Inside the car, it was completely silent. All the noise came from outside, a full-blown cacophony, voices clashing as each man tried to take control. Through the half-open passenger window, some reached for Regine's purse, their hands dirty, oily, and unwelcome. Others kept their eyes fixed on their weapons, as if weighing whether or not to squeeze the trigger.

I sat behind my cousin in that cramped two-door truck, my chest tightening with every breath. The space felt smaller by the second. Then came a single, unshakable thought. With gun barrels pointed like camera lenses and no room to run, I began to accept it; this might be the way I die.

"Turn here," one of them ordered loudly.

Having visited Cité Soleil multiple times before, I immediately recognized where we were being taken: Soleil 17, an overcrowded neighborhood with extremely narrow streets. My cousin and the driver had guns pressed against their temples. Two men jumped into the cab of the truck, both holding silver-colored pistols aimed directly at my head.

We had no choice but to comply. We followed their directions, turning into a narrow alley deep inside Soleil 17.

Every bump in the road jarred my body, but it was my heart that took the hardest hits. As we moved deeper into Soleil 17, I could barely breathe. I was sure I wouldn't be coming back out.

This is it, I thought. They're going to kill us.

I kept whispering to myself, dear God, don't let me see anyone I know. In my circle of friends and in the news, I had heard too many stories of kidnappings that ended in death once the aggressors realized the victim could recognize them.

After driving for about a mile, they ordered us to stop and get out. We stood against a cement wall; guns still aimed at our heads. Inside the narrow alley, one side was lined with concrete walls covered in slogans and messages of admiration for President Aristide. The other side was an open canal, clogged with trash, empty plastic bottles and mostly white Styrofoam containers.

"Give us everything you have," one of them demanded. The entire time, four men armed with pistols were rifling through our belongings, while a tall, skinny guy with a long gun stood a few feet away, keeping watch. He seemed to be the leader, dressed in a white ribbed tank top and cargo shorts, dripping with jewelry. He looked older, and it was clear that whatever he said would be the final word. We handed over all our money—mine, my cousin's, and the driver's. But it wasn't enough. They kept searching the car, convinced we were hiding more cash.

Then came a question that chilled me to my core. One of the men looked at the leader and asked,

"What do we do now?" Another responded coldly, "Should we just finish the whole thing so we can go?"

I froze.

They were talking about whether or not to kill us. The four men went back and forth, while the leader stayed silent.

The youngest one raised his voice, turning to the leader for direction.

"Chef, jwet pou ou wi. Sa ou di?"

"Chief, it's your call. What do you say?"

With the muzzle of his long gun resting near his sandals, the leader looked slowly from side to side, deliberate and unhurried, as if still weighing his options. He hadn't made up his mind yet, and he wanted us to feel that.

In those few seconds of silence, time held its breath. The silence stretched into more seconds. Each one dragged like an hour. It was clear the leader held the final word. Regine, the driver, and I stood frozen, eyes locked on him, waiting. The four young men barely glanced our way. They were too busy sorting through Regine's purse, picking through what was valuable and what wasn't.

Then, after what felt like forever, Regine spoke up.

"Could I get my driver's license, please? Please? It's useless to you. Please, guys?"

At first, I didn't even catch what Regine was saying. Her lips moved, and I thought I heard something about her driver's license came out, but my brain refused to register it. Of all the things to bring up in that moment, her license felt like asking for Wi-Fi in the middle of a flight emergency. But Regine's mind worked in straight lines, even in chaos. She was already fast-forwarding to the bureaucratic nightmare of replacing such an important document if she made it out of this kidnapping alive. Her request actually threw off a couple of the guys and gave me a second to breathe, but the leader didn't seem to care, not even a little. Still, fear kept boiling inside me with no sign of letting up.

One of them flung the license to the ground. It was his way of saying yes, but none of us dared to move.

Then the leader finally spoke.

"Let them go."

"Are you sure, Chief?" the younger one asked.

The leader snapped, "Yes! Leave them. Go! Go!"

And just like that, they spared us.

"Back out of here as fast as you can," they told us. "Don't talk to anyone. You hear me?"

Regine grabbed her license from the ground, and we scrambled into the truck. The driver threw it in reverse, speeding out of the slum and nearly crashing into a wall.

As we backed onto the main road, we came across a UN peacekeeping tank. Brazilian UN soldiers flagged us down.

"What just happened?" they asked.

It took me a moment to realize they were speaking English. I was struggling to find the right words. They had mentioned they spoke both Portuguese and English, since Regine and the driver didn't speak either, they left the talking to me. It felt like the gunmen hadn't just stolen our money, they'd robbed me of my English.

Still, I did my best to describe what the gunmen looked like, what they were wearing, what they told us, and how many of them had taken us. We were terrified to speak, but they insisted. Filing a report, they said, was mandatory. They escorted us into the UN tank. Inside, a handful of Brazilian peacekeeping soldiers lounged without a trace of fear. It felt like we had stepped into their small living room, snacks and drinks scattered around, as if this were just another day. Then I looked through one of the small, round windows, and my blood went cold. The same four gunmen had just stepped out of the alley. I could still see their faces, their clothes, the white ribbed tank top. Everything. I pointed them out to the soldiers.

"It's them! It's them!"

Regine leaned in to look through one of the portholes. She said just one word: "Jesus."

One of the gunmen spotted our truck parked beside the UN tank. He panicked. Then, suddenly, gunfire. The gunmen opened fire on the tank, and the UN soldiers shot back. Bullets rained down as the battle erupted. I had never seen or heard anything like it in my life. Each bullet hitting the side of the tank sounded like I was lying on a bed, head on a pillow, while someone made popcorn underneath. The sounds varied, some small and echoey, others loud and deep, like they could punch through the armored shell at any second. The tank never moved. The UN soldiers stayed in place, but their machine guns could swivel in all directions. Inside, the tank shook with every impact. Empty shell casings bounced around the floor, rattling underfoot. Some were so hot that if I didn't push them off my bare skin, they'd probably leave an unwanted tattoo. The gunfight dragged on, stretching time.

And then, just as suddenly as it had started, it stopped. The UN soldiers wouldn't let us leave right away; it was still too dangerous. Instead, they drove us about two hundred yards away before finally telling us it was safe to go. They retrieved our truck, handed us the keys, and told us to get as far away as possible. The truck had multiple bullet holes, a constant, haunting reminder of what we'd just been through.

We drove home in silence, still shaking.

"We shouldn't be alive," my cousin whispered. I didn't argue. That day, I had come face to face with death, and for reasons I still don't fully understand, I survived. Was it mercy? Was it grace? Or just luck? I knew it was grace. That day, death passed us by. But it left its fingerprints all over my memory.

CHAPTER 16

Mr. Nice Guy

By the time I was nearing graduation, I had started spending more time with missionary groups, gaining experience not just in speaking English but also in becoming a skilled interpreter.

The journey had been anything but easy, and learning English came with its fair share of embarrassing moments, some of which still make me laugh to this day.

People who are bilingual or polyglot know this all too well, but when you're learning a new language, certain words become your go-to, especially early on. Your go-to word is the one you reach for when nothing else comes to mind, a kind of catch-all. For me, that word was "nice." If something looked good, it was nice. If it was interesting, nice. If I didn't know the right word, I just called it nice. Nice had become my everything word. That habit led to one of my most embarrassing moments as an interpreter.

One of my first assignments was with a missionary group from Orlando, Florida. They were in Haiti for ten days, visiting a school and a church in the southern region. At the time, I wasn't the main interpreter. I was an assistant, tagging along to gain experience. My English was conversational, but I was far from fluent.

One particular Sunday afternoon, I made what I thought was a *nice* suggestion.

"Do you guys want to go see a cockfight?" Their faces went blank. One of them hesitated, then asked, "A what, Junior?"

"A cockfight! It's nice!" I repeated, beaming with enthusiasm.

I didn't realize that cockfighting was illegal in the U.S., or that most Americans viewed it as animal cruelty. In Haiti, cockfighting is as normal as a Sunday afternoon NFL game in America. It's legal and happens everywhere. People gather, place bets, and watch the fights.

In my hometown, it was just a part of life. But my mom hated it; she used to call the cockfighting rings *"the little church without a cross."* My siblings and friends often went, but I had no idea that in the United States, this was considered barbaric. I was simply trying to share a fun cultural experience. Instead of excitement, they looked horrified. One of them finally asked, "Junior, why do you want us to see this?"

I replied confidently, "Because it's a nice thing to see! I promise you guys will like it."

For years after that trip, my colleagues never let me live it down. They gave me a new nickname: "Mr. Nice Guy." Every time we saw each other, someone would joke, "Junior, have you seen anything nice lately?"

Looking back now, it's hilarious. But at the time? I wanted to disappear into the ground. It was a lesson in culture, language, and knowing your audience. Despite the embarrassing moments, I kept growing as an interpreter. Over time, I began earning money translating for various mission groups.

But one group always had priority—the missionaries from Minnesota. After all, it was one of them who had paid for my schooling, and I felt it was only right to always be available when they came to Haiti.

With every trip, every assignment, and every translation, my English improved. I wasn't just learning words; I was learning how to navigate between two worlds. Things were going well. But Port-au-Prince kept testing me.

One afternoon, I came within inches of being kidnapped. It was a Thursday afternoon, and I was walking home from school. I had no money for transportation, so I was heading back to Regine's house on foot. To pass the time,

I was listening to my Sony Walkman, tuned in to a radio news station. That's when I noticed it. A white Mitsubishi SUV was driving slowly behind me.

The road to Regine's house wasn't paved, just dirt and scattered rocks. Whenever a car drove by, I usually stepped aside to let it pass. But this one was moving unusually slow. I turned down the volume on my Walkman and listened. I could hear the tires pressing into the gravel, each turn kicking up dust and small rocks.

At first, I didn't think much of it. But then I realized it wasn't just driving slowly, it was watching me. Whenever I changed my pace, it matched mine. When I stepped aside to let it pass, it slowed down even more.

Something wasn't right.

My heartbeat kicked into overdrive as I picked up the pace. The SUV crept closer, narrowing the gap between us. Then the passenger door swung open, and someone jumped out, sprinting straight at me.

I didn't wait to see who it was. I ran. I ran like my life depended on it, because it did. I darted into a wooded area, weaving through trees and a sugarcane field, twisting and turning through the bush, trying to disappear into the forest.

Then I heard gunshots.

I don't know if they were shooting at me or firing into the air to scare me, but I knew one thing for sure: I had just escaped an attempted kidnapping. When I finally made it home, I was shaken but alive. Later that day, news reports confirmed what I had already suspected. There had been two kidnappings in the same area within hours of when I was nearly taken. Had I hesitated for even a second, I might have been one of them.

That was the moment I realized just how dangerous life in Port-au-Prince had become. It was no longer just about struggling to survive; now, staying alive was a daily battle. That night, I lay awake, replaying every footstep. Every sound in the street felt like danger breathing down my neck. With time, I grew brave enough to walk the streets of La Plaine again, but for many months, I left my Walkman at home. In a city like Port-au-Prince, people's eyes and ears don't work part-time. They are always on, scanning for danger and the unexpected.

CHAPTER 17
Before Dawn

While living in Port-au-Prince with Regine, I kept in close contact with my family back in Pianotte. Most of our calls happened late at night, between ten p.m. and five a.m. One of the two main cellphone companies in Haiti had instituted what they called 'Free Nights,' when calls within their network were free during those hours. I saved every conversation for the middle of the night. So, on February 18, 2006, when my phone rang after five a.m., I knew it had to be important because the call wasn't free. I just wasn't ready for the news it carried.

The call came from a neighbor, and his sigh told me more than his words ever could.

Before Dawn

"Hey brother, are you awake? Hey, listen… your father has gotten worse."

In Haiti, news of someone's passing is never delivered bluntly. The bearer of the message always tries to soften the blow. I immediately understood his tactic. This wasn't about my father's illness anymore. It was something much worse. I knew then that the end had come. By the end of the call, he finally spoke the truth: My dad had taken his last breath just minutes before the sun rose. For a man who lived by the belief that you should never let the sun rise before you, dying at dawn was his way of signaling he had crossed into eternity.

I was a hundred miles away in Port-au-Prince. I stuffed everything into a bag and prepared to leave the city, but I had no money for transportation. It's in moments like these that God provides. A few kind-hearted strangers helped me gather enough for the long journey back to Gris-Gris. The trip took more than eleven hours.

The air in Gris-Gris was heavy and smelled like sorrow. Neighbors were crying as I was nearing home. No one said it aloud, but I could feel their eyes asking the question I dreaded: Did he make it in time?

By the time I finally arrived home, it was already five p.m. My father had been buried.

Gris-Gris was a town without electricity, running water, funeral homes, or morgues. In places like ours, the dead cannot wait. There was a general, unwritten rule when it came to funerals: If someone died after one p.m., the body stayed in the house overnight, and the funeral was held the next morning. If someone died in the morning, they were buried the same day.

My father had passed away right before dawn, so by the time I arrived, he had already been laid to rest.

I never got to say goodbye.

The moment I saw my mother, she hugged me tightly. Her voice was steady but filled with sorrow.

"Sorry, we could not wait any longer."

Then she looked me in the eyes and said something I will never forget:

"But the good thing is, you will see him again. My only prayer is that it is many generations away. I know you will see him in heaven someday. But sorry, we could not wait for you to say goodbye." I nodded, trying my best to internalize her words. But inside, the pain of not seeing him one last time burned deep.

To this day, we do not know which illness took my father's life. We all knew he was sick, but medical treatment was a luxury we could not afford. He was just days away from turning seventy-nine years old. Did he die from natural causes? Or was it some undiagnosed illness that could have been treated?

One thing I've learned is that poverty and the unknown are cousins.

My mother was much younger than he was, and even though she outlived him, I knew she carried the weight of that loss every single day. But beyond the questions about his death, another pain lingered, one that still haunts me. One of the greatest regrets of my life is that I have no photos of my father. None.

If someone were to ask me, "What did your father look like?" I could describe him. But as the years pass, I find myself slowly forgetting his face.

The details blur, his expressions, the lines on his face, his big Barack Obama–like ears, the warmth of his eyes. It's all slipping away. He passed away in 2006, and at the time of this writing, it has been only 19 years. It wasn't that long ago. And yet, without a photo to hold onto, time is stealing his image from me.

There's more about my father in the chapters ahead. In fact, one of the main reasons I decided to write this book was to leave a trace, to do something my dad could never have imagined. Not having a way to see his face in pictures will always be one of my life's deepest regrets. But being able to tell stories about him, that, I hope, will keep his memory alive for generations to come.

A few months after my father's passing, I went back on a mission trip with the group from Minnesota. It wasn't easy. Grief was still fresh, but I knew the best way to honor him was to keep moving forward, to work harder, make something of myself, and take care of my family.

By that time, I was becoming more confident as an interpreter, no longer just an assistant, but the lead translator for many groups. Less than a year after his passing, I was fully back in the field, translating, leading, and building a future my father never got to see.

And so, I move forward.

Not just for myself, but for him.

PART THREE

No Grave for Grace

CHAPTER 18
A Woman Named Paula

Love was the last thing on my mind when I walked into the Matthew 25 Guesthouse that afternoon. But there she was, Paula, with a kind smile and a spark that would change everything.

She had traveled to Haiti to help with teacher training. As a special education teacher, she had so much to offer the educators in Gris-Gris. After a long flight from Minneapolis to Port-au-Prince, most missionaries spent the evening in the city before beginning the nearly one-hundred-mile journey to Gris-Gris. That evening when they arrived in Port-au-Prince, I stopped by the guesthouse to meet them.

That's where I met Paula.

It was a brief encounter, but I've never forgotten it. I couldn't explain what happened in that moment. I couldn't name it. But I felt it, something unfamiliar yet undeniable. A quiet certainty that Paula and I shared something.

When I walked in, she was sitting on the cement floor. That alone caught my attention. Most Haitians wouldn't sit like that. In Haiti, where water rarely flows from a faucet in people's homes, everyone tried to avoid sitting on cement floors to extend the number of days they could wear their clothes before washing. So, seeing Paula sitting on the cement floor felt like a small act of rebellion. It was such a simple thing, but it nudged something deep in me, a part of my heart I hadn't accessed before.

We spoke briefly. But I left with a feeling too real to ignore. Not the kind of thing you could describe in writing, but the kind of thing your soul tucks away. Some might call it love at first sight. I think it was more than that. I think it was divine.

I didn't let myself think too much about it at first. Most mission trip volunteers came to Haiti once and never returned. I didn't want to build expectations only to never see her again. A part of me wondered if I was crazy. A Haitian interpreter falling for an American teacher? It felt like something out of a movie, not real life. But every time she smiled at me, the world made just a little more sense.

As the days passed, we spent more time together in Gris-Gris, and I got to know her better. As an interpreter, I

143

worked side by side with her for a week. By the end of the trip, we exchanged contact information, though I still didn't know if I'd ever hear from her again.

A few days later, we started talking online, an hours-long conversation over Yahoo Messenger. At first, there was no plan, just two people who liked each other, trying to navigate what felt like an impossible situation. But as time went on, we both started wondering the same thing: Could we actually be together?

Six months went by, filled with phone calls, text messages, and dreams of what could be. We liked each other enough to take a risk. So we made a bold decision and planned to meet again, this time across the border in the Dominican Republic. Paula didn't come alone, though. She brought her sister and her sister's husband as backup, just in case I turned out to be a weirdo. I understood. It was a big risk for her to meet me again, and she wanted her family's approval. It was a big risk for me too. So we decided to share a once-in-a-lifetime gamble.

We spent another week together in the Dominican Republic, and by the end of it, we knew this wasn't just a passing attraction. We wanted to be together.

"What if I moved to the U.S.?" I said it before I even realized what I was saying. I'd made some big moves in my life, but this would be the biggest of them all.

We officially started dating long-distance, and a few months later, we met in the Dominican Republic again. By then, we were having serious conversations about the future.

We didn't have all the answers, but we knew we wanted to try. After less than fourteen months of dating, we made the decision that I would move to Minnesota. And so, the process began.

I opened up to my family and a few close friends about Paula, but in Gris-Gris and even in Port-au-Prince, her name was hardly spoken. I kept things mostly to myself. I was met with love and support from most of my family, but there were a few who had their doubts. And if I'm being honest, I didn't blame them. Long-distance love, especially one that involved two people living in two very different countries, was no small leap.

We applied for a fiancé visa. To make sure everything was handled properly, we hired an attorney to help us navigate the immigration process. Surprisingly, things moved quickly, less than eighteen months from start to finish.

The final hurdle? An interview at the U.S. Embassy in Port-au-Prince. Paula didn't want to take any chances, so she flew to Haiti to be there with me.

We arrived at the embassy and waited nervously, unsure of what to expect. As we passed through security, our minds were racing with thoughts about what came next. We waited for over an hour before our number was finally called.

The interview lasted less than four minutes. First question: "Where did you two meet?"

We both answered at the same time. Second question: "When do you want to travel to the United States?" One of us (I don't remember who) replied, "As soon as possible."

Then they took my Haitian passport and handed me a pink slip, a sign that my visa was going to be approved.

Paula flew back to Minnesota, and I stayed in Haiti for a few more months to prepare for the life ahead. A new country. A new beginning. A future I had never imagined.

In July 2009, I left Haiti for the United States. Destination: Minnesota. When I left Haiti, my heart felt like it had been tossed into a blender where sadness, fear, excitement, hope, and a few unnamed feelings were being thrown around. Living with Regine and her boys all those years turned them into more than just people I stayed with; they became *my* people. My family in Gris-Gris didn't know what to make of me leaving. This wasn't a vacation. This was the kind of goodbye that didn't come with a return date on a calendar. Going to a place I didn't know, to a family I had never met, and into a culture that felt foreign. Those kinds of goodbyes cut deep. Still, there was this quiet thrill in my chest about building something new with Paula. My heart was playing emotional tug of war and neither side was winning. I had dreamed of traveling to the U.S. for years to visit, but nothing could have prepared me for the shock of American life. And I wasn't coming to visit. I had a one-way ticket.

I arrived in Minnesota on a July afternoon, the heat settling around me as if it wanted to soften the shock of being in a place so unfamiliar. The temperature had less humidity than in Haiti, and I didn't need extra clothes to handle the climate in what was going to be my home away from home.

I was overwhelmed by convenience. Most immigrants would say they're overwhelmed by the grocery stores, the cereal aisles, the hot sauce selections, the endless variety of everything. For me, it wasn't just the stores. It was the convenience of everything.

I had spent my entire life in a place where water required a sixty-minute walk. Electricity was nonexistent. Simple tasks took an extraordinary amount of effort. For millions of Haitians living in Haiti, something as simple as boiling an egg can be as complicated as preparing dinner for a large group. They must first gather firewood and fetch water before they can even begin to cook.

Having water, not just for cooking and bathing but also for washing hands several times a day, was like a pipe dream. Water came out of the walls. Not just in the kitchen or the bathroom, a water spigot was even in the garage. Water could have been in every single room if you wanted it to be. That was overwhelming.

But there were a few discoveries that had completely jammed my brain. Let's start with TP. Toilet paper was the real shock. Not its use, I knew that part. But the endless choices. Grocery stores and gas stations alike offered more options than seemed necessary, in my opinion. Soft, ultra-soft, mega rolls, two-ply, three-ply, quilted, scented. It felt like choosing a mattress for your derrière. How much variety did people need?

The differences in lifestyle between the two countries were too many to list here. Life in Haiti and life in the U.S. felt like two different planets. On a map, Haiti sits only seven hundred miles from the shores of Miami, yet the gap between them seemed endless to me. Another discovery that didn't make sense was the United States Postal Service (USPS). I remember staring at the postal system here in awe. People would place a tiny square of paper in the top right corner of an envelope, drop it into a random metal or plastic box on the street, and somehow it would travel hundreds, even thousands of miles to land in someone else's hands. Back then, all of those miles cost the sender less than fifty cents. Back home, such a process would have been the equivalent of walking on water. In Haiti, the government postal service might as well not have existed. If a letter was urgent, the only way to make sure it arrived was to carry it yourself. When Paula and I started dating, she once sent me a package via USPS. To this day, I have never received it.

As an interpreter in Haiti, I worked alongside many missionaries from the U.S. I often asked them what they missed most about home. The answers were almost always the same: hot water and the freeway. I couldn't help but laugh. Hot water? I'd been taking cold showers my whole life. It had never even crossed my mind to want anything warmer. And the freeway? I was used to walking everywhere or squeezing into packed tap-taps. I couldn't imagine why anyone would miss a road.

But after a few years in Minnesota, I understood. Hot water wasn't just a luxury, it was essential. Driving on smooth, open roads felt like flying. I had taken for granted the things I grew up with, just as Americans take for granted the things they've always known.

Besides the convenience that surrounded my new life, I also noticed the hardworking spirit of the American people. It was common to meet individuals working multiple jobs just to provide for their families. In many developing countries, there's a myth that life in the U.S. is easy. But I quickly realized that while the country offers many opportunities, without hard work, those opportunities don't mean much.

Within just a few weeks of living in Minnesota, I came up with a phrase that still captures the stark contrast between my home country and the U.S.:

For most Haitians living in Haiti, life was easily hard. For most Americans living in the United States, life was hardly easy.

149

A Woman Named Paula

My first American meal was a cultural surprise. Before I left Haiti, I had never given much thought to American food. I assumed that wherever I went, I'd be able to find Haitian food or at least ingredients close enough. I was wrong.

My first meal in the U.S. was at my in-laws' house in Minnesota. Before the meal, my wife excitedly shared, "My mom is preparing an awesome meal for you, your first meal in Minnesota. It's a very Midwestern dish. You'll like it." I thought, maybe rice and beans? Maybe grilled chicken? Maybe salads, avocado, something familiar? Instead, I was served sweet corn and ribs. I was confused. Where I came from, boiled corn was a snack, something you ate on the go, not something you placed at the center of a meal. It was a quiet cultural surprise; one I hadn't prepared for.

Sixty-four days after my arrival in Minnesota, Paula and I got married at the Church of the Risen Savior, which was now my new church. My adjustment was going well.

But now, as I call Minnesota home, sweet corn and ribs have become my go-to when friends visit. What once felt foreign has become not only familiar, but a real favorite. Somewhere along the way, I settled into a life and a culture I never imagined.

I was a long way from Gris-Gris. A long way from my father's cornfield and my mother's kitchen. But somehow, in this land of snow and ribs, I had found a home.

CHAPTER 19

Behind Door Number One

Not long after settling in Minnesota, Paula and I sat down to talk about my future. The options felt limited, but I didn't believe my future had to be. There were two paths I felt drawn to.

The first was working with a nonprofit that served the less fortunate. Having grown up in deep poverty, I told Paula, "My dream job would be with a nonprofit. Even better if it helped Haiti."

I've always known I wanted to work in nonprofits because they were my kind of superheroes growing up. In Haiti, Non-Governmental Organizations (NGOs) and international groups like the United States Agency for International Development (USAID) were the quiet heroes behind the scenes. I got all my required vaccinations as a child thanks to USAID. In primary school, our school feeding program was made possible by the World Food Programme (WFP). Organizations like Catholic Relief Services and Food for the Poor always showed up like God-sent provisions in times of need. Their work didn't just make it possible for many to hope for a better tomorrow; in many cases, they made it possible for some to actually *see* tomorrow. So, choosing to work in nonprofits felt like my way of paying it forward, stepping into the shoes of those who once carried me through hard times.

The second field of work that really attracted me was law enforcement. I could picture myself in a uniform, serving and protecting. Paula didn't say much, but when I mentioned law enforcement, her eyes slowly drifted to the ceiling, as if she were praying for either patience or a change of mind.

No part of me grew up dreaming of wearing a badge. As a kid in Haiti, law enforcement wasn't about service or protection. It was about fear. My exposure was limited. In Gris-Gris, there was no police station. The punishment for stealing wasn't incarceration; it was humiliation and the inability to ever marry within the community.

In Port-au-Prince, the police were more focused on fighting gangs than on prevention or service. Whenever I saw an officer, I avoided eye contact. I just hoped I wouldn't be mistaken for a gang member. Theoretically, the police in Haiti had power. But rarely did they wield it for people like me. The little people. The poor. The powerless. It wasn't until I came to the United States, older and carrying a suitcase full of stories, that I began to see the badge as something else entirely. Not a symbol of force, but of opportunity. Of accountability. Of presence. And maybe, just maybe, of change.

In Haiti, the police force was militarized. Officers were sent wherever the government deemed necessary, often to the most dangerous corners of the country. If you didn't have connections with powerful people in government, you're likely to end up in the worst of those assignments.

I didn't have a mentor in the field in the U.S. What I had was a sense that I wanted to protect people who had no one protecting them. That idea, planted in me through years of watching my mother care for neighbors and complete strangers with nothing more than prayer and courage, followed me into this new life.

Somewhere between working night shifts and trying to get settled in a country that demanded so much from immigrants, I started asking myself a hard question: "What if I stepped into the very system I once feared and changed it from the inside?"

So, I made the decision that I would pursue becoming a police officer in Minnesota. The path seemed clear, so I started talking to people who knew more about law enforcement than I did. I enrolled in criminal justice and policing classes. Through those classes, I discovered a key difference between law enforcement in Minnesota and what I had seen in Haiti. Here, there were non-negotiable requirements before anyone could be trusted with a badge and a gun. First, I would need at least a two-year degree. Second, I had to be a U.S. citizen. I had no time to waste. I became strategic with the classes I chose, taking only those required for my law enforcement degree. In addition to learning U.S. laws and the Constitution, the classes helped me adjust to life in America. Somehow, I found them deeply satisfying. Maybe it was because, since my arrival in the U.S., I had become a news junkie. I watched everything, local, national, and international news.

News consumption was another difference between the U.S. and Haiti. In Haiti, news broadcasts were spaced hours apart, usually at eight a.m., noon, and four p.m. But in America, news flowed like water from a faucet. I immersed myself in it so completely that it became as much entertainment as information.

I binged the news like it was oxygen: CNN, FOX, MSNBC, ABC, CBS, NBC, and all the rest. I couldn't get enough. I was fascinated by the way a news network could take a single sentence of fact and stretch it into hours of conversation, each angle examined from a different lens. Something as small as a slight uptick in unemployment numbers suddenly became a multi-day story, with anchors, analysts, experts, and pundits all weighing in, each shading it through their own political beliefs. What struck me was that the interpretation became just as captivating as the news itself.

When I felt full from all the headlines and heated debates, I'd switch over to The Maury Show for dessert. Strangely sweet and sour, wild, uncomfortable, messy, and just distracting enough to keep me from thinking too much about home. I spoke with my family in Haiti sometimes once, sometimes twice a week. I missed them terribly. I thought phone calls would shrink the distance, but often, hearing their voices only transported my mind and soul back to Pianotte, while my body remained over a thousand miles away back at home in MN.

Back at the community college, I focused on my studies and barely made any friends. There were a few other immigrants from West Africa who shared my aspirations. We talked casually, but I wouldn't have considered them friends.

While I was tackling my criminal justice classes, I was also researching the path to becoming a U.S. citizen. I tried not to think too much about naturalization; my mind didn't have the memory space to process such a drastic change. After all, I didn't know anyone from Gris-Gris who had traveled to America and decided to change one of the things that made them proudly Haitian: the palm tree on the front cover of their passport.

Trading that for a passport with an eagle on the cover wasn't a step I was ready to consider. But I knew that if I wanted to wear a police uniform, I'd eventually have to face the reality of naturalization. Halfway through my criminal justice journey, I learned I had been granted legal residency, also known as a *green card*.

Just as I was adjusting to life in school and mapping out my future, life took a sharp and unexpected detour.

On January 12, 2010, just before five p.m., a 7.0 earthquake crushed my homeland, taking more than 300,000 lives in a matter of seconds. Nature struck without warning. It shook Haiti like a brutal and unforgiving punch in the gut.

I couldn't process it then. Even now, it feels unreal. For more than three days, silence met every attempt to call home. I feared that everyone I loved was gone. The earthquake happened on a Tuesday, and it wasn't until Friday evening that I finally spoke to my mom. I could barely hear her; our yard in Gris-Gris had become a gathering place where community members came to listen to the Word of God.

While the deadly quake shook the country, my mom was grounded in the Word, keeping Jesus as her compass. I remember vividly how that phone call ended. I was fighting back tears, trying not to let her hear the tremble in my voice.

I said, "Mom, I heard the city of Port-au-Prince was using large trucks and tractors to collect dead bodies and take them to a mass grave outside of Port-au-Prince."

She paused.

"Yes, that is what we're hearing too. But remember John 14. We are not going to be troubled. I know they are burying people all over Port-au-Prince. But here's the thing: God's grace is unchanging. Grace didn't die on Tuesday."

That statement didn't make sense to me at the time. But years later, I realized my mom was onto something deep. Her favorite word, *grace*, wasn't just a church word. She used it in good times and in hard times. In sickness and in health. In seasons of plenty and in seasons of lack. Grace, to her, was always enough.

I lost many good friends from school and from my English classes, including my favorite teacher, Mr. Cash. But life had to move forward. I took a semester off to grieve, then returned to school with a renewed sense of purpose to pursue what my heart desired.

I was taking classes with one magic number in mind: sixty credits. That was what I needed to be considered for the police academy. Mentally, I was ready. Physically, I was going to the gym five or six days a week. I was ready.

In April 2012, I reached the required sixty credits. My big yellow envelope was ready to be mailed to the academy for review. I remember it vividly. That Friday, I compiled all my documents, sealed the envelope, and sent it off to the Law Enforcement Center.

That Sunday at my home church, Risen Savior, I was just settling into my seat when a woman walked over and introduced herself. She said she'd heard about my background, how I came from Haiti and ended up marrying a Minnesota girl.

"I've been meaning to talk to you," she said. "I work for a nonprofit called Feed My Starving Children (FMSC), and there's an open position that made me think of you. Let me know if you'd like to chat after church."

Throughout the Mass, I kept thinking: What could this nonprofit be? She said the word "nonprofit." How did she know that was one of my two choices? Was God pranking me? I wished my flipped Nokia had internet so I could look up the organization and learn what they were about. While I was curious, I also knew I was just weeks away from entering the police academy.

After church, I connected with the parishioner again and learned that FMSC was a Minnesota-based nonprofit with a clear mission: *To feed God's starving children, hungry in body and spirit.* Founded in 1987, FMSC created a model where even children as young as five could volunteer for two hours at a time, packing meals for people in need. The meals were simple but powerful: rice, soy, dried vegetables, and a blend of vitamins and nutrients. As a Christian organization, FMSC welcomed hundreds of thousands of volunteers each year, all coming together for one purpose: fighting hunger around the world.

I went home and applied for the open position, which was a logistics coordinator role, handling food shipments to the Caribbean.

One afternoon, I made a trip to an FMSC location to see how they operated. When I arrived, I made a shocking discovery. My family had been recipients of FMSC food back in Gris-Gris. I had eaten that very food on multiple occasions. In fact, two years earlier, after the earthquake, FMSC had sent a 40-foot container full of dehydrated rice to my very community. How could this be? Whatever it takes, I would find a way to work for FMSC.

In the summer of 2012, I officially joined FMSC.

I decided to put my law enforcement aspirations on pause. Out of the more than 70 countries FMSC served, Haiti received the largest volume of meals. I was fully committed to FMSC and working full-time. The position allowed me to travel to Haiti and visit some of the people and communities receiving the food. For me, this job checked all the boxes. I loved what I did.

With a new job I loved came questions about where I was headed. I had already begun the process of naturalization, but in the nonprofit world and for the work I was doing, citizenship wasn't required. That left me with a choice. Should I move forward with becoming a U.S. citizen, or since I had stepped back from my law enforcement aspirations, should I set that process aside, too? These weren't small questions. They carried weight for the kind of future I wanted to build in Minnesota. After much prayer, I chose to move forward. I would pursue American citizenship.

At the start of 2012, the question of dual citizenship was everywhere in Haiti's news. That year's national elections saw several Haitian-Americans step forward as candidates for president. But there was a catch: Haiti didn't allow dual citizenship. Anyone with a U.S. passport was immediately disqualified from holding high office, including the presidency. For me, I had no political ambitions of my own, but the debate over citizenship was timely and impossible to ignore.

A new term began circulating among Haitians who had more than one citizenship. Many started referring to their U.S. passports as "administrative documents," an attempt to distance themselves from the accusation that they had betrayed their homeland. The Haitian legislature at the time felt the need to respond, so they amended the constitution. One word was altered: *renounce* became *repudiate*. The intent was to soften the meaning, to suggest that Haitians who adopted a new nationality weren't deliberately abandoning their Haitian identity, but rather having it rejected by law. To me, though, *renounce* had always sounded too harsh and final, too much like cutting ties or casting something off in shame, the way we speak of renouncing sin. Yet in the end, I felt the change was little more than wordplay. The heart of the matter hadn't shifted at all.

In February 2013, I raised my right hand, took the oath, and in that moment, I became an American. During the naturalization process, the U.S. government asked if I wanted to correct my name from Jignore to Junior. If I wanted to do it, that was my chance to make the change for free with the stroke of a pen.

I declined.

I became an American on paper, but not at the cost of erasing the boy from Gris-Gris. Jignore stayed. Asèn stayed. My roots stayed. I continued working for FMSC, and my new U.S. passport made international travel far easier than my Haitian one ever had.

Behind door number two was the fight against hunger. Behind door number one was a life in law enforcement. Both were about service. I chose the one with rice, soy, and vitamins, not the one with a badge, uniform, and firearm. I had no plans to change course. But if there's one thing my life has shown me again and again, it's this: Most of my major decisions have felt less like personal choices and more like executive orders, signed by God, with the ink of grace.

CHAPTER 20
Behind Door Number Two

My work at FMSC continued to flourish. Having been born into poverty gave me a strong frame of reference for the work I was doing. Growing up in Haiti, food was what my parents worked hardest for. We didn't have a rainy-day fund to draw from when times got tough; we worked hard just so we could eat.

That's why my role at FMSC felt so deeply personal. Every morning, I woke up looking forward to the day. The entire staff was laser-focused on the mission of feeding kids, and that kind of alignment made the work even more meaningful.

Over the years, I was promoted a few times, though each promotion kept me within the International Programs division. I remained close to the impact of the life-changing food we shipped to distribution partners around the world.

Even with that upward movement over the years at FMSC, there were moments when I felt a quiet pull, an urge to explore something entirely different: law enforcement. It wasn't something I could explain clearly, not even to myself. It was just a feeling I carried deep inside. I prayed often, asking God to take away the ambivalence I was feeling.

On one hand, I had a job I truly loved. Without a doubt, working at FMSC was the best job I'd ever had. On the other hand, the itch to shift directions wouldn't go away. I prayed for discernment, again and again, waiting for something concrete. But clarity never came. Instead, it felt like God was stirring the waters even more. Every so often, maybe once or twice a year, I'd catch this image in my mind—me in a police uniform, serving people in a way I hadn't expected.

What was missing from my life? I couldn't point to anything. In fact, FMSC gave me more than just fulfillment; it gave me proximity to home. On several work trips to Haiti, I'd extend my stay to drive out to Gris-Gris and visit my mom. That alone made the job feel like a dream. Most Haitians would give anything to have the opportunity I had. Yet the internal nudge toward law enforcement never faded.

So, I listened.

In 2019, I went back to school and earned a bachelor's degree in Criminal Justice and Leadership Management. With that new degree in hand, I reopened the door to the police academy. This time, I had everything I needed: a four-year degree and U.S. citizenship. So, I made the decision to begin preparing for physical training at the police academy. I also chose to keep my full-time job at FMSC. I was working while simultaneously taking policing classes and getting ready for the physical training at the police academy.

Though I had cousins in Haiti who were police officers, my understanding of the profession was secondhand at best and far removed from what I was about to experience. In this new country, I found myself learning the physical, mental, and cultural expectations of law enforcement.

That first day of training came with more questions than answers. One of the instructors took one look at me and said, "Big guys like you usually struggle here." At 5'11" and 228 pounds, I wasn't exactly small, and that comment weighed heavily on my mind. Was he right? Would I struggle? Was I not built for this?

His words lingered as I juggled the demands of a full-time job, police academy training, and my responsibilities at home. But I pushed through. I didn't quit, even though the strain rippled through my family. Training became a point of no return. It wasn't the physical demands that shook me; it was the mental load. The exhaustion. The relentless pressure of knowing I wasn't just showing up for myself.

I was also thinking about my wife, and I knew this path carried a weight neither of us had fully measured. While she supported me wholeheartedly, we both knew the path I was stepping into came with a strain unlike anything we had faced before. A career in law enforcement doesn't just shape the officer's life; it reaches into the home. Spouses carry that weight too, even without wearing the badge or walking the streets at night. I couldn't shake the pull I felt toward this work, but I also knew each decision I made would ripple through our family, pressing on her shoulders as much as mine.

On the first day at the academy, we were named Team 46. Getting my waistline measured, picking up my tool belt, and learning how to properly dress for training were all unfamiliar tasks. My body was there, but my mind was racing like a squad car in a hot pursuit. What if this is too hard? What if I can't finish? Still there I was, stepping into unknown territory with a low battery of courage, being drained by fear and doubt.

The first order of business was to elect a team leader. Given everything on my plate, including my demanding job with FMSC, I hadn't planned to volunteer. But no one else stepped forward. Eventually, I agreed on one condition: I'd share the role with a co-leader. I knew I couldn't lead alone.

I wasn't the oldest in the class, but I was close. Several of us were in our mid to late thirties, entering law enforcement as a second career or a calling we could no longer ignore. But we were training at a historic moment. I was in school preparing for the academy when George Floyd was killed less than 25 miles from where I lived. George Floyd's death on May 25, 2020, under the knee of Officer Derek Chauvin, reopened wounds in America that had never truly healed. The world erupted in protest. Minneapolis became the epicenter of a global conversation on police brutality. Should I even pursue a career in law enforcement now, at this moment, in this city? It felt like walking into the fire.

I avoided writing about the Floyd case in my criminal justice coursework. It was too raw. When people found out I was going into law enforcement, many were shocked. A Black immigrant man becoming a cop in Minnesota in the George Floyd era? For some, it was the typical "Good for you!" For others, it didn't add up. But for me, the George Floyd tragedy didn't make me quit; it made me double down. I wanted to become the kind of officer my community could trust.

Still, I found aspects of the training deeply unsettling. As I reviewed the curriculum, I noticed there were no classes on cultural awareness or differences. None. How could that be, especially in a state like Minnesota with the largest Somali population in the U.S.? How could officers effectively serve communities they didn't understand? I wasn't condemning the system, far from it. I was advocating for evolution. Officers should be trained to serve the communities they're sworn to protect, and that starts with cultural understanding.

Thanks to my international work at FMSC, I had experience engaging with a wide range of cultures. I had traveled to many countries and spoken with people from all walks of life. That perspective helped me adapt quickly. During one assignment, I wrote a paper on how eye contact was interpreted differently across cultures. One instructor said a lack of eye contact often signals dishonesty. I disagreed. Where I'm from and in many other parts of the world, making eye contact is actually a sign of disrespect. Cultural nuance matters. Policing can't be one-size-fits-all.

Despite the mental weight, I stayed committed. Being in the police academy in 2021 often felt like being a black sheep. Yes, there were people of color. Yes, there were women and men from different backgrounds in Team 46. But I still stood out. I was an immigrant. I had an accent. English wasn't my first or even second language; it was my third. I felt out of place.

A few of my fellow trainees liked to tease me, saying I was just doing this for fun. "You already have a dream job," they'd say. "Why trade that for a badge?" They weren't wrong about one thing: My job at FMSC was fulfilling. It allowed me to travel and experience the world in ways few people could. But for me, the pursuit of the badge wasn't about compensation; it was about passion.

CHAPTER 21
The Badge and the Burden

The first time I failed the shooting test at the police academy, I blamed fatigue. But deep down, I knew it was my friend's dream messing with my psyche.

I saw myself staying in law enforcement for a decade or more, maybe even for the rest of my working life. I pictured it as the profession that would carry me all the way to retirement. For many others in the academy, that kind of clarity wasn't there. In casual conversations, it became clear that some saw policing as a stepping stone, a temporary stop. But for me, it was the destination. Training was a real rollercoaster, full of ups and downs. Some days, I showed up excited. Other days, I questioned everything.

Two moments, in particular, shook my confidence in ways I hadn't expected. The first came in the form of a dream shared by one of my closest friends.

You know someone is a true friend when they're willing to bring something heavy to you, even when it's hard to say. About seven weeks into training, I got a text from a friend saying he had something urgent to share. When we talked, the first question he asked caught me completely off guard:

"Hey man, listen, when you train at the academy, do you guys use real firearms or fake ones?"

I told him we use both, real pistols at the shooting range and training weapons for role-play scenarios.

He paused.

"I had a strange dream about you, man," he said. "You were in a graduation parade with other recruits. You were the last one in line. When it got to your turn, the organizers ran out of uniforms. Everyone else got theirs, just not you."

He said no one seemed surprised. One of the instructors even grabbed the microphone and said, 'We still consider you a graduate, just without the proper tools and assignment.'

Then he told me what he thought the dream meant: Either I'd get injured or killed during training, or something would happen that would keep me from ever serving in law enforcement. Until now, I've never told anyone else about that dream.

This friend wasn't someone prone to dramatic visions or spiritual messages. In more than twenty years of friendship, this was only the second time he'd ever shared a dream with me. That made me take it seriously.

Growing up in Haiti, I was raised in a culture that paid attention to dreams. Still, I didn't tell anyone, not even my wife. I didn't want her to carry that weight. So, I carried it alone. The dream stayed with me. It haunted me. I became overly cautious at the shooting range. Small, routine mistakes started to trigger me. I began to overanalyze everything, my stance, my holster, even how I reloaded my magazines. I handled each bullet like it was a fresh egg, fragile and ready to break. The line between being careful and being paranoid started to blur. My confidence wavered, clouding my ability to make clear decisions. The fear that something might go wrong played on a loop in my mind. My accuracy slipped. Even the instructors noticed.

"Junior, what the hell is going on with you?" one shooting instructor asked. "You're usually more precise."

At the first shooting qualifier, I failed miserably. I needed a score above ninety percent to pass. I only managed sixty-six percent. That poor performance meant I had to retake it just a few days later. No one knew about the dream, but they could tell something was off.

Every shooting night, I had three words I'd say to myself to boost my confidence: *Bring it on*. But after hearing about my friend's dream, my inner confidence was as off target as my aim.

Eventually, I pushed the dream to the back of my mind. By the halfway point in training, I was shooting well again. But the fear never completely disappeared; it just tucked itself behind the routine.

I threw myself into the training and did my best to keep things steady at home. I started buying books for my wife about how to cope with the stress of being married to a police officer. Between my full-time job, the evening and weekend training, and family life, I was stretched thin. Time with my children slipped away into the margins of my schedule, bedtime stories replaced by night drills and crime scene studies.

But they found a way in. They got curious. On the rare days I didn't have training, dinner as a family was extra special. Often, the kids would ask, "Dad, what did you learn today?" It wasn't just small talk; they genuinely wanted to see it. On weekends, if I wasn't too drained, we created our own mini academy at home. I'd show them how to do proper takedowns or how to conduct a safe search. They loved it. It became our little tradition. That year for Halloween, my son Wesley dressed up as an FBI agent, complete with a vest, badge, and gear. Seeing that, I realized just how much they were soaking in from my journey. All through this time, I kept the dream tucked away like a stone in my pocket.

At the academy, two events live rent-free in every trainee's mind: getting tased and getting pepper-sprayed. They are rites of passage. For most people, those were the big hurdles. But I had a third one: that dream. Getting tased, getting pepper-sprayed, and wondering if the dream would come true.

One drill brought me straight back to Haiti. We practiced live scenarios all the time, but the one that stuck with me most was how to conduct a proper traffic stop. It seemed routine, but we were taught how quickly it could turn dangerous. I understood the weight of that lesson. What I didn't realize was how soon or how often I'd be tested on it.

CHAPTER 22
Triggered by a Traffic Stop

Cover and concealment weren't just technical terms that we needed to master at the academy. They were like the gospel. Preached and drilled until they settled deep into our instincts. One hides you. The other shields you. Both could save your life. But the more I heard those words, the more they began to mean something else.

My doubts were concealed behind my gray uniforms and shiny training shoes. The quiet mind wrestling stayed hidden behind the steady face I wore during roll call. The training belt I strapped on each day held more than flashlights and handcuffs. It carried the weight of questions I hadn't spoken out loud. My body was being shaped for duty, but my mind was patrolling the perimeter of the academy, unsure. Somewhere outside those walls, I was still deciding if this was the right move.

In my humanitarian world, I spent my days strategizing about the best way to feed people, praying with them, and listening to stories that often didn't make news headlines. FMSC had been a calling, and I was doing deeply meaningful work. This new world, waiting for me a few weeks away, was giving me a different kind of language: investigations, interrogations and traffic stops. Even the seemingly small things, like writing a speeding citation, had the potential to change in the blink of an eye and become a deadly force encounter. And there I was, still wondering if I belonged in the uniform at all.

According to the United States Bureau of Justice Statistics, over twelve million traffic stops are conducted in the U.S. every year (Bureau of Justice Statistics, 2024). At the academy, they drilled into us the importance of treating each stop with caution and precision. Many police departments across the U.S. even removed the phrase "routine traffic stop" from their vocabulary. There's no such thing as a routine stop, they said. Every stop carries the risk of danger. I was about to find that out firsthand.

During one training session, it was my turn to perform a simulated traffic stop. An active-duty officer played the role of the driver. I followed protocol: initiated the stop, turned on my flashing lights, and radioed dispatch. The driver did exactly what I hoped, slowed down and pulled over safely. So far, so good. But before I could even assess the situation, the door flung open. The driver jumped out with a weapon drawn and pointed straight at me.

Time stopped. My mind shut down. Blank. Even though I knew we weren't using real firearms during training, my body couldn't tell the difference.

I couldn't hear anything. It felt like the world collapsed around me. I jumped out of the training car instinctively, without putting it in park. My patrol vehicle slowly rolled away as I scrambled for cover.

For a moment, I wasn't in Minnesota anymore. I was back in Cité Soleil. Soleil 17. That training weapon pointed at me had unlocked something buried deep. I wasn't reacting to the role-play anymore. I was reliving the moment I was held at gunpoint in one of the most dangerous neighborhoods in Haiti. My body responded before my mind could.

It was embarrassing. My classmates got a good laugh out of it. They had no idea what was happening inside me. I never told the instructors. I didn't want to explain that I was dealing with unprocessed trauma. I didn't want to seem weak.

But that day made me realize just how much I had compartmentalized over the years. That moment didn't just shake me as a trainee; it cracked open years of memories I had tucked away just to keep functioning, both at work and in life.

I recovered, eventually. I got back on track with training, at least on the outside.

Meanwhile, back at FMSC, I kept quiet about my transition. Only my closest colleagues knew. I didn't want to create confusion or become a distraction. I remained committed, planning to take a few weeks off after graduation before leaving the organization in the spring or early summer of 2022.

A major leadership transition was also underway at FMSC. The Vice President of International Programs, my department head, was stepping down after fifteen years. Just as I was nearing graduation from the police academy, the organization was preparing for its annual partner conference in South Florida. The conference is a gathering that brings together humanitarian organizations from around the world. Over the course of two days, participants receive practical training and up-to-date information relevant to the humanitarian field. My department was responsible for organizing the event, and I couldn't miss it. Not only was it an important moment for the organization, but it would also be my supervisor's final conference.

I requested a week off from the academy. I knew missing a week of training in a six-month program was risky, but giving a proper farewell to a mentor and friend who had given fifteen years of service mattered more. I flew down to Florida.

At the start of the conference, I stood quietly in the back of the ballroom. As worship music played, I closed my eyes and thanked God for the journey I'd had at FMSC, nearly a decade serving children across the globe. It was the best job I'd ever had. I whispered to myself again and again, "Thank you, Jesus, for such a beautiful ride."

Tears welled in my eyes. I stepped out of the ballroom, overwhelmed. Outside, I ran into a colleague who knew about my plan to transition into law enforcement. He looked at me with intensity and said, "Just so you know, this is not your last conference. You were made for this work."

Those words hit me harder than I expected. Somehow I could tell they weren't just pleasantries; they were coming from deep within.

That same week, the job listing for the vice president role was still open but about to close. I had ignored it. I had no intention of applying. But something had shifted. Throughout the conference, people came up to me, unprompted, and encouraged me to apply. Some said it casually. Others were adamant. Slowly, the idea began to settle in my heart.

Throughout the conference, my mind kept drifting back to a dream a colleague had shared with me nearly eight years earlier. In her dream, our current vice president had retired, and I had stepped into his role as the new leader. At the time, we laughed it off. I wasn't even thinking about promotion. But now, that dream resurfaced.

I began to pray, asking God whether He truly wanted me to pursue law enforcement. Again. That night, I called my wife and asked, "Okay, I know this is a crazy idea…but what if I applied for the VP role at FMSC and didn't pursue law enforcement?"

She paused, then said, "Wow! That would be really different... But, honey, you gotta do what makes you happy."

Still unsure, I prayed for clarity. That night, sleep kept its distance. I tossed and turned for what felt like hours, trying every mind trick I knew to shut my thoughts down. Nothing worked. Eventually, I reached for my phone. Normally, I'd play a familiar podcast to help me drift off, but this time, I opened YouTube and clicked on a random suggested video. It was a motivational speech by Les Brown. While the name was familiar, I didn't recall ever listening to him before, but his voice filled the hotel room like a wake-up call.

The entire talk was about taking risks in life. It felt oddly specific, almost too perfect. I turned up the volume, wide awake, listening to words that stirred something in me instead of helping me sleep. I sat in that hotel bed, torn. Part of me felt like applying for the VP role at FMSC would be quitting on the law enforcement dream. Another part whispered, what if this is obedience, not quitting? About halfway through the video, I heard a quote that jolted my brain:

"Most people fail in life not because they aim too high and miss, but because they aim too low and hit."

The next morning, I applied for the VP role.

The job had been open for many weeks. Three days after I submitted my application, it closed. A few weeks later, I was offered the role of Vice President of International Programs at Feed My Starving Children. Days later, I graduated from the police academy.

It was surreal. Two dreams had intersected: my journey in law enforcement and my calling in humanitarian work. My friend who had shared that unsettling dream called and said, "I told you. You were never meant to be a police officer." And the colleague who had dreamt of me stepping into leadership? She just smiled.

At the time of this writing, I lead an incredible global team at FMSC, doing meaningful work around the world. When I look back over the thirty-eight years of my life, the word that echoes the loudest is grace.

How does a boy from a poor village in Haiti grow up to help lead a global effort against hunger, a cause he knows all too well? How could a recipient of FMSC meals come to lead the international division, overseeing the very food he once received in Haiti? How does a boy who once missed important exams because he couldn't afford the required twenty cents grow up to become an author? The answer is simple: grace. I know I am under God's grace. And I know you are, too.

I believe you are part of a bigger story, one filled with grace, pain, resilience, and purpose. Just like mine. Grace doesn't vanish when life gets hard. Even when struggles roll in seemingly without end, grace is still present. It stands like a shield, keeping us from shattering. A life overflowing with blessings is grace, but so is a life pressed by problems after problems, stacked high like the mountains of Haiti. Grace is found in both.

A life of hardship and discomfort isn't a life to run from. It's a life that stretches us, strengthens us, and ultimately shapes us into who we were meant to be. We live in a time when social media pressures us to showcase perfection, to curate a version of ourselves that appears flawless. But I've come to understand something important: A perfect life with no wrong turns, no doubts, and no pain might sound appealing, but that's a *fictional life*. On the other hand, a life that moves forward even when fear is close. A life that sits with questions, holds hands with doubt, and still finds its way to joy. That kind of life isn't perfect, but it's a *functional life*. Don't get the two mixed up. Let your life be functional. Remember, perfect and real aren't synonyms. Let your life be real, not perfect. Let it be messy, honest, and brave.

CHAPTER 23
A Photographic Memory

Culture is invisible, like air. It's present in every moment, shaping how we move and speak without us even realizing it. I've always believed that learning a new language is much easier than learning a new culture. You can memorize vocabulary. Culture has to be absorbed.

It's in how people gather around food, how they show respect, how they handle joy and loss. You hear it in a laugh. You see it at a glance. Culture speaks in gestures, in timing, in what's assumed and what's left unsaid.

One of the most hilariously curious cultural differences between the U.S. and Haiti is the concept of time, or perhaps the complete rejection of it. In America, being "on time" is practically a moral virtue, with people scheduling coffee like it's a NASA launch, nearly synchronizing their clocks to arrive at the same moment.

But in Haiti, time is more like a suggestion, gently waved at from across the street. A two p.m. meeting might start around three, maybe four, and no one blinks. In fact, if you show up on time, you'll likely be sitting alone, wondering if you misunderstood the invitation.

It's only after living in Haiti for a while that you would begin to embrace what locals call *'Haitian time'*, a philosophy that suggests, with great charm, "Relax, life will happen when it happens." Or, as most people say, "As long as it's the same day, relax."

After spending years in Minnesota, I've noticed a slow drift away from *Haitian time*. I didn't plan it, and I wasn't trying to let go of it. But the pace of life here has a way of shaping you; it pulls you in. At first you think you're just adjusting, but before long, you find yourself fully immersed, keeping up with a culture that runs on speed and precision.

At the time of this writing, I've lived about forty-five percent of my life in the U.S., one of the wealthiest countries in the world. The remaining fifty-five percent was spent in what many call the poorest nation in the Western Hemisphere. That split is more than just numbers; it's a lens I carry. It colors the way I see the world and the way I tell my story. I've lived in both extremes, and my life will always reflect the pull of both places. I see it like a battery, with two distinct poles connected for a purpose. One carries the charge, the current that drives things forward. The other holds the counter-voltage, essential for balance, for calibrating the right amount of output. You need both for power to flow.

This dual perspective has shaped my worldview, as well as the writing of this book itself. For example, the first few chapters were written while visiting Haiti. Others were shaped in Africa. A dozen or so pages came together over the Pacific Ocean, in seat 41J on Delta Airlines during a trip from the Philippines. Most of it was written in a quiet suburb just outside the Twin Cities of Minneapolis and Saint Paul. Growing up in Pianotte, I never imagined writing a book, and I certainly didn't imagine writing it across several continents. But life doesn't always follow our plans. It usually unfolds in unexpected ways.

If there's one thing I've learned, it's that life moves forward, whether we want it to or not. People come and go, memories fade, and time erases even the sharpest details. We believe we'll always remember, but the truth is, we forget. And that's why I write. We must leave a record of our lives on this earth.

One of my greatest regrets is having no pictures of my father. All I have left are stories, memories, and fragments I've worked hard to keep alive. Without photographs, my mind has struggled to hold on to the image of his face and the sound of his voice, the way his hand felt patting my head, the sight of his smile, the feeling of his arm around my shoulder.

I tell my children about him all the time, about his strength, his resilience, his wisdom. But when they ask, "What did Grandpa look like?" I have no way to show them. That reality weighs on me deeply. If I could trade anything to give my children just one glimpse of their grandfather, I would.

But growing up in Haiti, taking pictures was a luxury we couldn't afford. In a town of 16,000 people, there were fewer than four photographers. And they weren't there to capture birthdays, weddings, or everyday life. Their cameras were reserved for official business, school IDs, national registration, passports, and government paperwork. In fact, I can count on one hand the number of pictures that exist of me as a teenager.

So when I think about leaving a trace, I think about all the people, like my father, whose stories fade into time without a single image or record left behind. I think about how many lives are lived and forgotten, not because they weren't meaningful, but because no one had the necessary means to preserve them. This book is my trace. My way of saying I was here and a way to preserve my parents' stories as well.

Halfway through writing this book, I decided to share the news with my department at FMSC. I work with a group of energetic, exceptional individuals who are kind and passionate about feeding hungry children. If you've ever come across the term *'Minnesota Nice,'* it's more than just a saying to these people. These folks aren't just about the label, not the fake, half-kind version mixed with a hint of passive-aggressive undertone. No, they embody the real, genuine, and truly gracious kind.

As a team, it's not uncommon for us to have deep, honest conversations about life, family, and faith. Several of them knew that not having a picture of my dad was a scar I'd carry until the day God calls me home. What I didn't know was that some of them had quietly decided to offer me the kindest gift I could ever have imagined. They had concocted a secret plan: to give me a memory of my dad. They were determined, and they went all in. They hired the world's most accomplished forensic artist to draw a sketch of my dad. I didn't know what to make of the news when they shared it with me.

I was floored.

Within weeks, I was connected with the sketch artist, Lois Gibson. She holds the Guinness World Record as the most successful forensic artist in the world. She's known globally for her work, and her passion comes from a place of deep, personal pain.

After surviving a near-death experience as a young woman, she made it her mission to help others find justice. Her sketches have led to the capture of over 1,300 wanted criminals. She's worked with countless police departments and federal agencies. She's received award after award.

But this time, her work wasn't about solving a crime. This time, it was about bringing back a face that had slowly begun to slip from memory. A face I hadn't seen in nearly twenty years. A face that would become not only a treasure for my fading recollection, but a gift for my children and their children.

So we met over Zoom. From the very beginning, I could tell that what Lois possesses is more than just a skill. It's a gracious gift from the Master of the Universe. She was just as excited as I was to bring my dad's image to life.

"Alrighty, let's go," she said with a smile.

She began asking me questions about my dad's features, what I remembered most. A few days earlier, she'd sent me a catalog of headshots and asked me to pick the ones that matched his features as closely as possible. I assumed she'd take a few days to work on the sketch. I was wrong. This was going to be same-day delivery.

As we chatted casually over Zoom, she was already drawing. It didn't feel rushed or mechanical. It felt like two people walking down memory lane, pausing now and then to admire the flowers, the cracks in the road, even the chipped paint on old fences. There was no interrogation, just conversation.

Every so often, she'd switch topics. She told me about her most memorable cases, the awards she'd won, and the stories behind her work. Her humor was sprinkled throughout, painted right into her words. She kept reassuring me. "I'm so excited to give you a photo of your dad. You're going to like it." I was drawn in, not just by the sketch, but by her story. After just eighty-seven minutes, Lois showed me the following sketch.

Silence.
I was blown away.

At first glance, it was just a resemblance. But then I looked again and I saw him. I saw Accevil. I saw the man who raised me. The man who worked so hard to feed me. The man who poured himself into me.

My heart, which had been racing, almost stopped.

I felt relief.

I felt something I hadn't felt in a long time. Something deep. Something I can't fully explain here, but it's alive inside me.

To those of you who helped make this possible, you know who you are. Thank you.

These kinds of gestures are rare. I hesitate even to call this a gift. It's more than that. It's a piece of life.

The gift of remembering someone we often take for granted is quiet, but powerful. Today, with all the technology at our fingertips, we mostly rely on photos and videos to hold onto memories. Most people can scroll back and see a face or hear a laugh. I couldn't. But Lois's sketch stirred something in me. It brought back a few memories of my dad, faint but familiar. The kind of memories that surface right when I need them most. And by "memories," I mean two small, seemingly insignificant moments I've stored in a special folder in my mind. Moments that feel like they're tucked away inside a password-protected file somewhere in the cloud storage of my memory. I revisit them when I need to feel close to him again.

The two moments that mean the most to me are simple, imperfect, unplanned memories that have become my treasured possessions.

The first is the story of *The Wrong Shirt*.

One Sunday morning, my father rushed to get ready for church. He wasn't the type to go often, but my mother never let up in her mission to get the whole family there. Little by little, he was becoming a familiar face at Saint Rose of Lima, though no one could match the devotion of my mother. But on that particular day, my dad hurried out the door without much thought. A few of us even joked that maybe he thought he was headed to what my mom called *the little church without a cross*: cockfighting.

At church, my brothers and I noticed something was off. He was wearing my mother's shirt. It was just a bit too tight, with the buttons on the wrong side, a clear sign it wasn't made for a man.

Later that morning, back at home, the teasing started the moment he walked into the yard. We were already laughing before he even realized something was up. He looked puzzled and annoyed.

My brother Claudy laughed, "I wonder how many people thought you were Sister Esther today, dad."

For weeks, months, even years, we teased him. My father, always serious, tried to hide his amusement. He wanted to be mad, but even he found it funny. That ridiculous,

189

accidental moment became one of my strongest memories of him. It reminded me that beneath the stern determination it took to raise a fine family, he had a sense of humor, too.

The second memory is one I call *The Cake Incident*.

In 2002, my home church, St. Rose of Lima, was celebrating its fifth anniversary as an official parish. The priest invited the entire town to a celebration designed to thank God for the newly founded parish. Of course, no party in Haiti was complete without rice and beans.

It was a grand occasion; there was food, music, and something rare for us: dessert. Not desert, but the kind of food you eat after you've eaten.

Every guest received a slice of cake wrapped in a thin napkin. My father, unfamiliar with this tradition, was so focused on enjoying his cake that he didn't realize he was also eating the napkin along with it. One of my older brothers noticed, and within minutes, the incident was leaked to the rest of the Obrand crew. Right away, we knew this was going to make headlines in the Obrand household. My brother Claudy didn't see it happen in real time, so we made sure to report every detail to him.

Claudy was the lead teaser in the family, and we knew this incident was too good not to place in his hands. He knew exactly how to start the teasing and how to time it. He was an expert at bringing it up when you least expected it, yet somehow, it always fit the moment. If Claudy lived in the U.S., he'd be a top-notch roast comedian. He'd make millions.

Now that the church celebration was over, the real fun was about to begin.

"Dad, I need proof you didn't eat the napkin. Show it to me," Claudy said in his most serious tone.

But, of course, he had no napkin to show. For weeks, we laughed, especially when my brother Claudy would randomly blurt out, "Hey, Dad, where's your napkin?"

For years, we remembered and relived that laughter. There were even days we joked about trying rice and napkins instead of rice and beans. We found creative ways to poke fun at him, and his annoyance only fueled our teasing.

Neither of these moments was planned. They didn't come from vacations or grand events, luxuries we couldn't afford. They were everyday mistakes, small joys that grew into something much bigger.

That's the true nature of the best memories: you don't create them by planning. Life just hands them to you, a gift to treasure for a lifetime.

Growing up in Haiti, we never went on family vacations. There were no photo albums filled with snapshots of trips to sandy beaches. What we had instead were long afternoons of laughter, games in the yard, and the kind of moments that stitched us together. Those were some of the best times of my childhood. My childhood in Haiti was indeed filled with questions, about life, about suffering, about God, about community. It was a world where faith was both a comfort and a test, where spirituality was woven into the very fabric of existence.

Creating memories is one of the easiest and least expensive things you can do. In fact, some of the best memories you'll ever create are completely free. So please don't make the mistake of overcomplicating what it means to create memories. And don't be surprised if your most meaningful ones come when you least expect them, like a shirt worn by mistake or a napkin accidentally eaten with a slice of cake. Perfect memories don't come from perfect moments. Rather, they come from being fully present in imperfect ones.

My life has unfolded in ways that, statistically speaking, are highly unlikely. I've had the privilege of guiding you through some of the most complex, difficult, and unbelievable chapters of life in one of the poorest countries in the Western Hemisphere.

Though my limited view of the world as a child often led me to question everything, I'm now certain of one thing: It was God's grace that kept me safe through close encounters with danger, brushes with voodoo, and the long, winding pursuit of success in America.

I don't share these stories to evoke pity or make you feel sorry for my family, especially those still living in Haiti. My reason for sharing my highs and lows is simple: I hope it gives you a window into what life is like for millions around the world who've lived stories similar to mine. It's also my sincere hope that this book has inspired you and moved you to take action. If you're a person of faith, I hope it has strengthened your beliefs. If you're not, I hope it made you pause and reflect. No matter what you believe, there's something undeniable about the way life unfolds, the way paths open, the way moments align, and the way we survive things we once thought would break us. That is no accident. That is grace. And grace will never be buried in a coffin.

Conclusion

I hope this book has given you something to hold on to about life, spirituality, and culture. Sharing my story wasn't easy, but it was necessary. We all have a story, and one of the greatest mistakes we could make is to take our stories to our grave with us. As you reach these final pages, I'm honored that you've come this far. I want to leave you with a challenge:

What will your legacy be?

What you choose to do now, in this very moment, can outlive you. Whether it's through words, photographs, acts of kindness, or the lives you touch, I urge you to please leave something behind.

The idea of writing this book lived in my heart for many years. At first, it was only a distant thought, but over time it grew into a mission I could no longer put aside. Now, as I arrive at the final pages, I find myself asking you the same question I asked myself at the beginning: *What would you do if you knew you couldn't fail?*

If no answer comes right away, don't give up. Ask again. Ask often. Ask the person you are now, the person you hope to be, and the one you are becoming. If you keep asking, clarity will rise to the surface. And when the answer stirs something deep within you, don't turn away from it. Please do it. Leave a trace. Don't let *'someday'* become the graveyard of your dreams.

It's a truth we all must face: One day, your name will become history. Your face will fade from memory. Your voice will be forgotten here on Earth. There may come a time when no one alive will remember what you sounded like. So, what will you do today to make sure that doesn't happen?

I suggest we each take time to create memories, capture stories, and leave a trace. I know your dreams might feel overwhelming at times, like they're bigger than anything you think you're capable of. If you're someone who feels intimidated by the size of your aspirations, consider my story. I never imagined that one day, you'd be reading my words. But life turns a new leaf every second, and with it, so does your capacity to pursue what God created you for.

When you dream about what's possible for your life, remember this: There is one ingredient that preserves every dream, it's grace. And because of grace, your dreams don't expire. You decide when they bloom.

I urge you: Live a life that impacts as many people as possible, in ways that matter. Don't hold back. You've got what it takes. Even when the road ahead feels uncertain, trust yourself. Life on this side of eternity is short, but it is also a gift. If you choose to view life through that lens of urgency, you'll begin to recognize the moments that seem too perfectly timed to be mere coincidences.

If you're reading this as a believer, I pray my story has deepened your faith and reaffirmed what you already know to be true. If you're reading this as a skeptic, I hope it has encouraged you to pause, recenter, and consider that there may be more to life than what meets the eye.

My mother has taught me to see life as a journey, a short layover on the way to something greater. Through that lens, I picture all of us on the same flight. It's true I've been given a little more legroom, or maybe by God's grace, I was moved to a different seat. But make no mistake, I am not exempt from turbulence or rough air. True success isn't about where you're sitting on the plane. It's about how you treat the other fellow passengers and whether you take joy in the journey. It's also about holding onto the hope that there is a destination ahead. Some of us travel light, others don't. But if you see this life as a layover, you'll find it easier to face the bumps, the sudden shakes, and even the hard landings.

Sharing my story with you was never about proving I climbed some ladder of success. You might look at my life and call it a success story, but for the most part, it isn't about the upward mobility that unfolded through these chapters. My life indeed looks very different now compared to the days I spent in Gris-Gris. Every time I visit my family back in Haiti, I can feel the shift in power dynamics since moving to the U.S. But deep down, I am still the same boy who used to kick soccer balls, barefoot, made of banana leaves wrapped inside an old sock.

Growing up poor had shaped me. It taught me how to see people. Now, living as a middle-class American, I carry that early experience like a tattoo on my spirit. And I've come to understand something even deeper: Poverty isn't simply the absence of money. Some people are so poor, all they have is money.

As you turn the final page, I hope that your faith has been renewed, your heart opened, and you've witnessed that your life is neither random nor accidental. It is part of something far greater than you can imagine.

Maybe you came to these pages full of faith, or maybe you came full of doubt. Either way, pause for a moment and see the bigger picture. You were made with intention. With purpose. With love. You were made by His grace.

Time is a gift we unwrap every single day. Unwrap it with intention. Unwrap it with gratitude. Unwrap it knowing that what you leave behind may one day be all that remains.

Give the gift of your story. Let it be passed down and remembered. Time itself is grace, because as long as breath fills your lungs, you still have time. Time to act, time to forgive, time to speak the words waiting inside you.

Grace is the gift no one can buy. It is not earned. It is given. And it was always meant for life, not death. Grace has no price tag, no borders, no conditions. And grace certainly has no grave.

Epilogue

A Land too Rich to Be Poor

Haiti is often portrayed as the poorest country in the Western Hemisphere, a label repeated so often that it has become part of its identity. In fact, throughout this book, I've used that very phrase multiple times when referring to my home country. But is that the whole truth? Is Haiti defined only by its struggles?

Growing up, my friends and I often repeated a well-known saying: "Haiti is too rich to be poor." It wasn't a phrase we coined ourselves. It's as popular as rice and beans, heard in songs, poems, and everyday conversations among Haitians. It may sound like a contradiction, but if you understand Haiti beyond the headlines, you'll see the deeper truth in those words.

Yes, Haiti is poor in infrastructure and, perhaps, in opportunity. But it is rich in history, culture, resilience, and untapped potential.

It is a country with deep spiritual roots, vibrant traditions, and a people who, despite unimaginable hardship, never stop fighting for a better life. The struggles you hear about: earthquakes, hurricanes, political instability, poverty, coups, and gang violence, are all real. But they are not unique to Haiti. These challenges exist in different forms all over the world, in both developing and developed nations.

Take superstitions, for example. They're often associated with Haiti in a negative light, but don't they exist everywhere? In the U.S., many buildings skip the 13th floor because it's considered unlucky. In various cultures, Friday the 13th is viewed with fear. In Italy, placing a hat on a bed is seen as a sign of death. In Austria, some believe eating a strange combination of garlic and yogurt brings luck. In Egypt and many other places, opening an umbrella indoors is said to bring bad luck or can even be considered an insult. These beliefs may look different from one culture to another, but the concept is the same: Superstition is universal.

Yet many people, especially outsiders, insist on tying Haiti's struggles to voodoo. I can't count how many times I've heard someone said that Haiti's problems are the result of a so-called "pact with the devil." This belief is so widespread that, even after the 2010 earthquake, global conversations claimed the disaster was divine punishment for Haiti's spiritual history. Remarkably, a 7.0 magnitude earthquake that took the lives of more than 300,000 people was seen by some as God putting His foot down.

This narrative was repeated in all sorts of spaces, from church services to television interviews, from international NGOs to dinner-table conversations.

Was the 2010 Haiti earthquake a direct result of voodoo? I can't answer that question. Did Haiti really make a pact with the devil in exchange for its independence? I can't answer that question with a simple yes or no, but allow me to give you my honest take.

To understand this fully, we have to go back to 1791 where a secret gathering of enslaved Africans marked the beginning of Haiti's revolution against France. It was on the evening of August 14th, more than twelve years before Haiti gained its independence, that a voodoo ceremony at Bois Caïman in northern Haiti became, in the eyes of many, the spark that ignited the country's fight for freedom.

The ceremony, led by a voodoo priest named Boukman and a Mambo (a voodoo priestess), was a spiritual gathering where the enslaved called upon ancestral spirits and vowed to fight for their freedom. Blood sacrifices were made, including that of a black pig, an act that held deep spiritual significance in African traditions.

Haiti would go on to abolish slavery in a way no other country had. Led by Jean-Jacques Dessalines, the Haitian army fought against Napoleon's troops and, on January 1, 1804, declared its independence.

For many Haitians, this moment is remembered as a powerful symbol of resistance, courage, and the unyielding desire to be free. But for others, especially outsiders, it's often viewed through a darker lens, as the moment Haiti *'sold its soul,'* sealing a fate of endless struggle.

But is that correlation, or causation?

Haiti's independence came nearly thirteen years after the Bois Caïman ceremony. So, did voodoo play a role in Haiti's revolution? That depends on whom you ask. What's undeniable is that Haiti won its freedom at an unimaginable cost, one that France and other Western nations never truly forgave.

If you were to ask most Haitians about the country's ongoing struggles, they would undoubtedly tell you that Haiti has been treated unfairly by many nations around the world. The blood of Haitians was spilled across the land in the fight for liberty. And though I know I'm biased as a native Haitian, I truly believe Haiti's story is one for the books. It's a country that achieved something in 1804 that no other Black nation on earth had ever done: A successful slave revolt that led to independence. It was, and still is, a remarkable story with an unanticipated ending. A small army of enslaved people defeated the mighty Napoleonic forces. Haiti became a symbol of freedom.

Yet instead of honoring Haiti as a beacon of Black liberation, many have twisted the story, painting it as something born of darkness rather than of the bravery of ordinary people. I'm not naïve. I know there are dark forces in Haiti. In fact, I've shared several stories in this book about the thick, oppressive weight of voodoo and how deeply it's intertwined with daily life there.

Nonetheless, I have a hard time believing that every setback, every hardship, every wrong turn, every disaster, or every painful crash can be blamed on a single voodoo ceremony from 1791. In my opinion, such thinking would be discounting God's miraculous, redemptive power.

Haiti's wounds run deep. It's a country that can't seem to catch its breath. The disasters come in waves, which is why the Haitian proverb goes, "Behind every mountain, there is another mountain." Human hands craft some of these disasters; others are born of nature. And of course, some have deep roots in the spiritual realm, too.

It's easy to look at Haiti's ongoing struggles and think, this has to be more than a coincidence. But is it really? Do Haiti's hardships come from a spiritual curse, or are they the direct result of centuries of economic exploitation and political mismanagement? There's no denying it, Haiti often feels like a country trapped in a loop of crisis, as if someone hit repeat and walked away.

The man-made disasters strike first: political chaos, widespread corruption, and the assassination of sitting presidents, the most recent being Jovenel Moïse in July 2021.

Kidnappings tear families apart. Cholera outbreaks steal the lives of the most vulnerable. And the ever-tightening grip of gang violence keeps the capital, Port-au-Prince, in a state of constant fear.

Then, just when it seems things might calm down, Mother Nature delivers her own blows. Earthquakes flatten entire cities and kill thousands. Hurricanes rip through already fragile homes. Floodwaters rise and wash away the few who dared to rebuild.

Haiti's problems are many, and the truth is, we Haitians have played a major role in creating and perpetuating some of the challenges we face today. I'm not here to point fingers only at outside forces like the international community. That would be an oversimplification.

Yes, you'll easily find Haitians who blame every misstep and hardship on outsiders, especially Western nations. But I believe that kind of thinking is one-dimensional. It leans into a victim mentality and can become a shield that excuses our own wrongdoings. The reality is far more layered than that.

There are many factors at play and plenty of hands in the mix. You can't understand Haiti's struggles by looking through a single lens. Some root causes can be traced back generations before mine. Others stem from the ongoing mismanagement and malpractice shaping the country today. Together, these forces paint a fuller picture and bring us closer to answering the question: How did we get here?

Back in the 1940s, Haiti was a tourist destination. We were also one of the world's top coffee exporters. Our mountainous terrain produced some of the finest beans anywhere. But by the 1980s and 1990s, as internal struggles deepened, those same mountains became less productive and more symbolic of our uphill battles.

The choices made in the 1950s and 1960s have rippled through time, and we're still living with the consequences today. Haiti was once called the *Pearl of the Antilles*. I'm reminded of that every time I spot a Haitian license plate. As the first Black independent nation in the world, pride runs deep in our veins.

In just fifty years, Haiti experienced two drastically different political systems. When my dad married my mom in the late 1960s, the country was under the tight grip of a dictatorship. François and Jean-Claude Duvalier, father and son, ruled Haiti for nearly thirty years. In fact, when I came into the world in 1984, we were still living under that iron-fisted regime.

François "Papa Doc" Duvalier ruled Haiti from 1957 to 1971. Under his regime, Haitians lived in fear. Dissent was dangerous. His government created a powerful and deadly paramilitary force known across the country as the *Tonton Makout*. Their job was to track down anyone perceived as an opponent of the regime and eliminate them. They weren't afraid to carry out killings in broad daylight.

Duvalier (the father), a graduate of the University of Michigan with a degree in public health, was a renowned medical doctor. That's where the nickname "Papa Doc" came from. But alongside his medical training, he was also a devoted practitioner of voodoo, which added an eerie layer of power and fear to his rule. After he died in 1971, his son, Jean-Claude, known as "Baby Doc", took over.

Baby Doc became known for his lavish lifestyle, funded by the people's money. While many Haitians saw him as less brutal than his father, his regime was still responsible for the deaths of thousands and the looting of the nation's resources. His extravagant wedding in the 1980s, which reportedly cost around two million U.S. dollars, shocked no one as he had a well-earned reputation for living large.

Under the Duvaliers, Haiti was slowly bled dry. A small elite grew wealthy, while the majority of citizens sank deeper into poverty. By 1985, the people had had enough. They began organizing and rising against the regime. In February 1986, after a massive popular uprising, Baby Doc was overthrown. He fled into exile in France. With assistance from the United States, he boarded a U.S. Air Force plane, reportedly taking millions of dollars with him.

After more than two decades in exile, Baby Doc returned to Haiti in 2011. He was arrested and charged with embezzlement and human rights violations. Three years later, the man who once ruled with wealth and power died of a heart attack. He never truly faced justice, at least not in the way justice was meant to be served.

After Baby Doc exited the country, a new term entered Haiti's political vocabulary: democracy. It marked a slow but deliberate shift from dictatorship to something entirely new. We had to at least try.

In 1990, Jean-Bertrand Aristide became Haiti's first democratically elected president. But even that historic moment came with chaos. He never finished his first term. Political pressure from both within Haiti and the international community forced him into exile in the United States. He was later brought back in the mid-1990s.

Aristide was elected again in 2000, but once more, he couldn't finish his term. He was forced into exile for a second time, again with help from Western nations. As we tried to embrace democracy, the pride of being the world's first Black republic began to feel chipped away. It felt like we were caught between two worlds, and neither seemed to offer the answers we needed.

On one hand, many of Haiti's most stable years occurred during the dictatorship. Under the Duvaliers, the country was, in some ways, safer, cleaner, and more prosperous, at least on the surface. But gatherings of any kind were forbidden. The government saw them as threats. Back then, freedom came at a cost. And sometimes, people paid with their lives.

Today, freedom exists on paper, but safety comes at a premium. The country is poorer, more fragile, and undeniably more dangerous. Millions of Haitians would return to the Haiti of the 1970s and 1980s in a heartbeat, even if it meant giving up some of their freedoms. That's how desperate things have become.

Haiti has been called many things: the poorest country in the Western Hemisphere, a failed state, a nation cursed by its past. I'm not here to dispute those claims. I'm asking you to widen your lens.

I'll say it again: Haiti is too rich to be poor. That might sound contradictory, maybe even absurd, given Haiti's well-documented struggles. But the richness I speak of goes beyond money, infrastructure, or political stability. Haiti's true wealth lies in its people, its culture, its history, and its resilience.

Yes, Haiti faces enormous challenges. Yes, it has endured suffering and never-ending instability. But our richness is measured by how many times we rise after being knocked down.

At the time of this writing, Haiti is living through one of the darkest seasons in its history. Gang violence has displaced nearly a million people. Hunger affects more than half the population. For years, the country has been governed by interim administrations. Every elected position is vacant. Elections are long overdue, and the resources needed to restore order are scarce.

Still, I've always resisted the idea that Haiti is uniquely doomed. The struggles we face, poverty, corruption, natural disasters, and political unrest, are not ours alone. These problems exist in different forms all over the world. Yet Haiti is often singled out as cursed.

That word, curse, gets used too often. It can become a distraction. It pulls attention away from the complex reasons behind our long road of hardship. It overlooks the systems, the decisions, the history, and the choices that brought us here, choices made both within and beyond our borders. Let's take a deeper look at some of those choices.

1. Haiti was economically strangled from the start.

After Haiti won its independence in 1804, France forced the country to pay for lost *'property and wages,'* money France claimed to have lost because enslaved people had become free. This so-called "independence debt" totaled more than 150 million francs and crippled Haiti for over a century. It drained the nation's wealth and kept it financially dependent on foreign powers.

Haiti didn't have a choice but to pay up. There was no social media campaign to spark outrage. No hashtag to raise awareness. No allies to stand with us. Haiti quietly paid millions to France simply for gaining its freedom. The final payment on that absurd debt was made in 1947, two years after my mother was born. Imagine winning the World Cup or a Super Bowl championship as an underdog, then being forced to pay the losing team, because they felt embarrassed and had already printed championship shirts. Not only are you covering their losses, but you're also paying for their emotional damage for generations after the game.

That's what Haiti lived through, except it wasn't a game. Our freedom came at a cost to our oppressors. And that cost was rolled into a literal payment plan that stretched over a hundred years. In recent decades, many Haitian presidents have tried to bring this issue back to the world's attention. Jean-Bertrand Aristide made it a central point of his second presidential campaign. You could see it everywhere: banners in major cities, radio ads across the country. By the early 2000s, most Haitian third graders could recite the amount France owed to Haiti.

After the 2010 earthquake, President Michel Martelly revived the call for restitution. Then, in 2015, former French President François Hollande made headlines when he publicly acknowledged that France had a debt toward Haiti. It was a simple truth, but he was the first French president to say it out loud. President Hollande concurred that Haiti has not been treated fairly and acknowledged that France "owed a debt to Haiti." He spoke those words just before boarding a flight to Haiti to meet with President Martelly. His words sent shockwaves through Haitian communities everywhere.

Many believed that if he was bold enough to say those words before arriving in Port-au-Prince, he must be preparing to make a major announcement once his feet touched Haitian soil. But when his plane landed, and he spoke again, he added just one word to his previous statement: moral.

Yes, moral.

"France owed a *moral* debt to Haiti," he clarified.

A sneaky, diplomatic move.

That one word changed everything, and not in a good way. For many Haitians, myself included, it felt like a gut punch. A diluted truth. A way of saying, "We see your pain, but don't expect anything tangible."

2. The world turned its back on Haiti.

Western nations, including the United States, France, and Britain, saw the emergence of a successful Black republic as a threat. After Haiti gained independence in 1804, these nations refused to recognize it. Many of them, especially France, punished Haiti for its victory over slavery by cutting it off economically. They refused to trade with Haiti, isolating it from the global market.

During the era of the so-called "independence debt," France wasn't alone. It had powerful allies. Haiti had none. France led a not-so-subtle campaign to prevent Haiti from being seen and acknowledged as a legitimate, free Black nation.

That campaign worked. Western countries followed France's lead and turned their backs on Haiti.

The United States, for example, didn't officially recognize Haiti's independence until 1862. If you're doing the math in your head like I was, let me help you: that's fifty-eight years after Haiti had already declared itself free. And it wasn't because the U.S. hadn't heard the "breaking news" on January 1, 1804. Haiti is only seven hundred miles from the shores of Miami. I guess a nation of formerly enslaved people overthrowing a European power was too dangerous of an idea.

As a result, Haiti was locked out of normal trade with much of the world for decades. Its independence wasn't celebrated; it was treated like a warning. These early years of isolation and economic punishment weren't just moments in history; they helped shape some of the struggles Haiti still faces today.

3. Haiti's political class has been plagued by corruption.

Perhaps Haiti's biggest enemy over the past several decades has been the deep-rooted corruption embedded in its political system. While every country deals with corruption to some extent, in Haiti, it has seeped into nearly every corner of public life.

The Duvalier regime, from 1957 to 1986, was especially destructive. The father-and-son duo drained the country's limited resources for their own gain. Millions were stolen from the public and funneled into private bank accounts (Abbott 1988, 143).

I've already shared details about the extravagant lifestyle of Baby Doc, but he wasn't the only one. Too many Haitian politicians began their careers as poor, ordinary citizens and, within months, became inexplicably wealthy. That wealth often comes at the expense of innocent Haitian taxpayers. I personally believe part of the problem lies in the population's tolerance for corruption, something that can be traced back to three main factors.

a. First, the lack of access to education. The Haitian Constitution promises free primary education, much like what exists in the United States, but that promise rarely becomes reality. When a nation is less educated, corruption tends to thrive. I'm not saying there are no educated people in Haiti; there are many. However, the system as a whole doesn't foster or reward education. Without widespread access to knowledge, corruption finds fertile ground to grow. Also, in recent years, many educated Haitians have been fleeing the country in search of a better life abroad. A phenomenon better known as a *brain drain*.

b. Second, Haiti lacks the infrastructure needed to build national unity and accountability. This one is harder to explain, but I've seen how it plays out firsthand. Growing up, I never paid taxes, not because I was dodging them, but because the system to collect them simply didn't exist. The only taxes I ever paid were those included in the prices of food we bought. There were no property taxes. No income taxes. But then again, there was no income anyway. My father built his house on his own land and didn't need a construction permit from the government. We didn't pay for electricity, because we had none in our village. We never gave the government any money directly. And in return, we rarely received any kind of government assistance as a family. We always saw the government as a faraway system, meant for other people, not for us. In that kind of environment, it's hard to feel like a stakeholder in the national system. When politicians steal money, it feels like they're stealing from the country, but not from *my* own pocket. In contrast, here in the United States, people pay taxes on nearly everything: income, property, clothing, and even lottery winnings. There's a direct connection between my contribution and the national budget. But in Haiti, that connection is often missing. As long as people feel disconnected from the system, there will be a kind of passive acceptance of corruption. Until there's both a system and a mindset shift, corruption will likely continue to thrive. Until Haitians can clearly see that the money being siphoned off by politicians is their own, corruption will keep its grip. Until there is a justice system that sends a clear message, one that holds the powerful accountable and defends the poor, it will not be fixed. Justice is not just a concept. It is the surest antidote to corruption.

c. I've made it this far without even mentioning the dark forces of spiritual warfare at play in Haiti. But we can't explore Haiti's struggles without at least bringing the spiritual headwinds to the surface. Somehow, Haiti is tied to voodoo in a way that is hard to untangle. Haiti and voodoo go hand in hand, and in my opinion, that's not a good thing.

It's not my intention to condemn those who practice voodoo. One aspect of voodoo that has sparked heated debate among Haitians everywhere is whether it is more cultural than spiritual. The answer varies depending on who you ask. From a cultural lens, no culture is necessarily better than another; they're simply different.

When the French brought enslaved people from Africa to the Americas, those individuals brought with them their practices and beliefs, including voodoo. In Haiti, not everyone practices voodoo, but many acknowledge its presence. So, in one sense, you could argue it is cultural. Some parents, even those who consider themselves Christians, still follow traditions such as giving their children "good luck baths":

rituals involving leaves and herbs meant to protect against bad spirits.

My family didn't practice voodoo, but I grew up surrounded by it. In fact, one of my uncles was deeply involved, though he never openly admitted to being a voodoo priest. In our village, voodoo wasn't something people declared openly; it was simply understood (or suspected). I remember nights sitting around after dinner, listening to stories about spirits, curses, and spells. To us, those stories were real; we had seen firsthand how they manifested.

Growing up in Haiti, my exposure to media was extremely limited and vastly different from that of children in the United States. While American kids heard ads for fast food chains, video games, or the latest consumer goods, the airwaves I listened to were filled with a very different kind of marketing. Many of the commercials were either loosely or directly tied to voodoo, offering promises of wealth, luck, protection, and even invincibility. These messages weren't whispered in secret; they were proudly broadcast over the radio and, occasionally, even on television. A lot of Haitians believed them, or at least took the chance that they could change their lives.

It was common to hear bold claims from spiritual leaders promising to shift fortunes, bless businesses, heal sickness, or even guarantee lottery wins. Many people, desperate for a better life, would save what little they had just to visit these so-called powerful figures in hopes of a breakthrough. Some believed so deeply in these promises that they would turn to voodoo priests before seeking medical care, financial advice, or legal help.

To outsiders, this might seem strange, but the truth is, these belief systems were deeply embedded in everyday life. Even those who considered themselves Christian often walked a fine line between faith and superstition. Some would pray in church on Sunday and still seek a voodoo priest's blessing for good fortune on Monday.

I was always fascinated by some of those advertising claims. The get-rich-fast schemes always came with a caveat. A voodoo priest could make you rich, but it might shorten your life. Or they could predict future lottery numbers, but you'd have to pay an outrageous amount of money.

Recently, many voodoo priests have taken to the airwaves across Haiti to protest gang violence and call for justice. But if they are truly so powerful, why haven't they used their influence to stop the gangs that have been terrorizing the nation for years?

These questions have often shaped and strengthened my faith. Despite growing up around voodoo, I believe my faith in God is stronger today because of it.

Let me be clear: I'm not here to say voodoo is all an illusion, far from it. The forces of voodoo are alive and real in Haiti. They can do things that defy logic. But they have limits.

They can't cross the line or alter God's plans. In my experience, voodoo is more of a distorter than a constructor.

One of the most well-known voodoo priests in Haiti over the years was Ajimal, a name that literally translates to *'evil act.'* His reputation stretched across the country, and he was known for offering his services not just to everyday people but especially to the powerful. Unlike many local voodoo practitioners who served their communities, Ajimal was a priest almost exclusively for the elite, politicians, businessmen, and those in positions of power.

For decades, presidents, elected officials, and wealthy individuals sought him out, believing he could protect them, guide their decisions, and help them hold on to power. His influence ran so deep that his name alone could spark fear across the nation.

But after years of serving as a priest who mediated with ancestral spirits, Ajimal converted to Christianity. His conversion was, in itself, a powerful story, one that revealed the might of God. After his transformation, Ajimal's sermons quickly became some of the most widely listened-to messages in Haiti, not only because of who he had been, but because of how candidly he spoke about the hidden world of voodoo.

He spoke about the dark forces of voodoo in a way only someone who had lived within them could. With a haunted, unflinching honesty, never boastful, Ajimal admitted he had once wielded powers that defied logic. He claimed to have placed spells that bent people's wills, summoned spirits that tormented the living, and even turned people into animals, something that might be dismissed as myth in the West but carried a chilling plausibility in Haiti.

Ajimal was, without a doubt, a vessel for evil spirits in Haiti. During his years as a voodoo priest, he often spoke about certain people who seemed untouchable: individuals who disrupted his rituals, causing his spirits to become dull and inactive, even from a distance. He referred to them as the *'real Christians.'* He had tried to cast spells on Christians, but something always went sideways. After his conversion to Christianity, he realized what had been happening all along: It was the power of Jesus.

So, do voodoo spirits have power? Yes. But does that power have limits? Absolutely. Above all, the power of Jesus surpasses every other spiritual or earthly force in the universe. I don't just believe this, I know it.

On one hand, voodoo's limited but real power has contributed to Haiti's struggles. But on the other hand, the fear surrounding voodoo may have caused just as much damage, perhaps even more. One thing I've learned is that fear is a powerful force, and those who control fear control people. Fear makes people believe that someone else holds the key to their success. It convinces them to spend their last savings on rituals instead of investing in their future. Fear drives people to seek quick fixes rather than real, lasting change.

But faith is stronger than fear. Faith doesn't demand money for miracles. It doesn't offer false promises in exchange for devotion. Faith doesn't control; it frees.

Looking back on my childhood, I can now see that God was always present, even in the midst of confusion, deception, and hardship. Throughout this book, I've shared personal stories, historical reflections, and cultural observations to help you see Haiti beyond the headlines. My goal hasn't been to tell you what to believe, but to invite you to look deeper, to see Haiti for what it truly is, not just what casual observers say it is. I ask you to reconsider the myths that have long surrounded my homeland. Haiti is not just a struggling nation; it is also a country of resilient, hopeful, and resourceful people.

Faith is not just about religion. It's about choosing truth over fear, hope over despair, and purpose over deception. Life isn't as simple as it appears on the surface. There are forces we don't fully understand, and there are battles we don't always see. But through it all, one truth remains constant: God is greater than fear, greater than struggle, and greater than anything that tries to control us.

I do not doubt that some of the stories I've shared on these pages might seem like myths to you, or maybe even downright illogical. Honestly, I wouldn't blame you. There are things logic simply can't explain, no matter how hard we try. I also know that some of you might read certain parts of this book and think, *that's just something that happens in Haiti, in those places steeped in dark voodoo and old-world spirits.*

If that's your mindset, then you're mistaken. Evil doesn't care about geography or wealth. It doesn't only linger in the corners of impoverished nations where heritage and ancestral beliefs collide.

As a follower of Jesus Christ, I carry a deep concern for others who share that faith, especially when it comes to how we view the devil. The devil isn't stupid. In places where survival is a daily battle, he offers false promises that prey on desperation. But in wealthier, industrialized countries like the United States, where most people don't worry about their next meal, the devil uses different tactics. He distracts us with what's shiny, easy, and fleeting. He makes us restless, dissatisfied, and more dangerously, he gets us addicted to things that poison our hearts and numb our souls.

So, is Haiti "cursed?" Or has it simply been dealt a terrible hand, shaped by centuries of exploitation, isolation, and mismanagement, rather than a mystical tie to dark spirits or voodoo? It's easier to blame a religion of spells and curses than to confront the harsh truths of history.

Haiti is not cursed. It is tested, and so are we all. Struggle does not define us. What defines us is how we choose to move forward: with faith, with resilience, and with the belief that even after the hardest battles, there is always another mountain to climb.

If you've made it to this paragraph, you've reached the end of my book. It has been an honor to have shared my world with you. My sincere hope is that you've found at least one meaningful takeaway from my life journey. Whether you are a believer, a doubter, an explorer, or even a denier, my story is, in some way, your story too. When I pause and reflect on everything I've been through, there's only one explanation: God's grace. If there's one thing Haiti has taught me, it's this: Grace doesn't check ID before it is unlocked and poured. For what the world called buried, grace called planted.

About the Author

Junior Obrand was born in Gris-Gris, a rural village southeast of Port-au-Prince, Haiti. The eighth of ten children, he grew up on the receiving end of humanitarian aid, an experience that shaped his deep commitment to service.

In Haiti, Junior worked as a translator, helping connect American missionaries with local communities. After high school, he moved to the United States and earned a bachelor's degree in Criminal Justice and Leadership Management.

Today, Junior serves as Vice President of International Programs at Feed My Starving Children, one of the largest Christian volunteer-based nonprofits in the U.S. In this role, he leads global food distribution efforts that reach children in over a hundred countries worldwide. His perspective is grounded in lived experience—once a recipient of aid, now a leader in delivering it.

Junior lives in the Twin Cities of Minneapolis and Saint Paul, Minnesota, with his wife and their two children.

For more information, visit juniorobrand.com.

Junior and his wife Paula

Junior and his cousin Regine

Junior pictured in training gear - First week of police
training

Esther Jacotin pictured inside her home church of St. Rose of Lima in Gris-Gris.

Church of St. Rose of Lima in Gris-Gris.

References

Abbott, Elizabeth. *Haiti: The Duvaliers and Their Legacy.* First edition. New York: McGraw-Hill, 1988.

Burnette, Bobby, and Sherry Burnette. *Love Is Something You Do: The Extraordinary Journey of Compassion and Faith.* 35th Anniversary Edition. Whitaker House, originally published circa 2014; revised and expanded edition.

Bureau of Justice Statistics. 2023. "Contacts Between Police and the Public, 2022." U.S. Department of Justice. Accessed September 3, 2024. https://bjs.ojp.gov/press-release/contacts-between-police-and-public-2022.

Chomsky, Noam, Paul Farmer, and Amy Goodman. *Getting Haiti Right This Time: The U.S. and the Coup.* Common Courage Press, September 2, 2004.

Collège de France. "Haiti, 1825: From Independence to Debt." Symposium organized by Antoine Lilti, Collège de France, January 12–14, 2025. Accessed April 11, 2025. https://www.college-de-france.fr/en/agenda/symposium/haiti-1825-from-independence-to-debt.

Katz, Jonathan M. "The Ransom: How a French Bank Captured Haiti." *The New York Times*, May 20, 2022.

https://www.nytimes.com/2022/05/20/world/americas/haiti-history-colonized-france.html.

Les Brown. "Why People Fail." YouTube video, 18 years ago (published March 8, 2007). https://www.youtube.com/watch?v=uekdv8SiTec.

McFadden, David. "French President Makes Unprecedented State Visit to Haiti." *AP News*, October 1, 2013. https://apnews.com/general-news-30b36c857ad541cca9570330cf11ac79.

New York Times. 2014. "Jean-Claude Duvalier, Haiti's 'Baby Doc,' Dies at 63." *New York Times*, October 5, 2014. https://www.nytimes.com/2014/10/05/world/americas/jean-claude-duvalier-haitis-baby-doc-dies-at-63.html

Office of the Press Secretary. "Statement by the Press Secretary." *The White House*, September 20, 2004. Accessed March 7 2025. https://2001-2009.state.gov/r/pa/prs/ps/2004/29990.htm

Schomburg Center for Research in Black Culture, New York Public Library. "Duvalierist Government Collection, 1958–1989." *Archives & Manuscripts*, Schomburg Center for Research in Black Culture, NYPL. Call Number Sc MG 733. Accessed December 12, 2024. https://archives.nypl.org/scm/181329.

Tapp, Susannah N., and Elizabeth J. Davis. *Contacts Between Police and the Public, 2020*. Bureau of Justice Statistics report NCJ 304527, U.S. Department of Justice, November 18, 2022. https://bjs.ojp.gov/press-release/contacts-between-police-and-public-2020.

About Feed My Starving Children

Feed My Starving Children (FMSC) is a Christian nonprofit organization with a mission to *feed God's starving children, hungry in body and spirit.* Volunteers and donors fund and hand-pack nutritious, dehydrated meals made of rice, soy, vegetables, and essential vitamins. These meals are then sent to FMSC's distribution partners who serve in some of the world's most food-insecure communities.

To volunteer or donate, visit: fmsc.org

One Book One Meal

Hunger is not an inconvenience; it's a killer. Let's help hungry children turn the page on hunger. For every copy of this book sold, a donation will be made to FMSC to help fight world hunger.

No Grave for Grace

www.ingramcontent.com/pod-product-compliance
Lightning Source LLC
Chambersburg PA
CBHW021223130626
46554CB00004B/1342